Write Deep, Believable Characters

Karyn Henley

Andon Press
Nashville, Tennessee

Copyright © 2014 Karyn Henley

All rights reserved. No part of this publication may be reproduced, distributed or transmitted in any form or by any means, including photocopying, recording, or other electronic or mechanical methods, without the prior written permission of the publisher, except in the case of brief quotations embodied in critical reviews and certain other noncommercial uses permitted by copyright law. For permission requests, write to the publisher, addressed "Attention: Permissions Coordinator," at the address below.

Andon Press
www.andonpress.com

Book Layout ©2013 BookDesignTemplates.com
Cover image © KeithBishop/istockphoto.com
Enneagram image ©PeterHermsFurian/istockphoto.com

Writing Deep, Believeable Characters/ Karyn Henley —1st ed.
ISBN 978-1-933803-62-3

Contents

1. Creating Characters 1

Part One: Making Characters Act Their Age

2. A Brief Overview 11

3. Infants: Birth to Two – Trust vs. Mistrust 17

4. Early Childhood: Two and Three- Autonomy vs. Shame 25

5. Early Childhood: Four and Five - Initiative vs. Guilt 35

6. Six Through Nine – Industry vs. Inferiority 41

7. Tweens: Ten Through Twelve – Industry to Identity 49

8. Adolescence: Thirteen to Twenty – Identity Formation vs. Identity Confusion 59

9. The Twenties: Intimacy vs. Isolation 71

10. Thirties through Sixties: Generativity vs. Stagnation 77

11. Older Adulthood: Integrity vs. Despair 79

12. Practical and Cultural Considerations 83

Part Two: The Enneagram for Writers

13. Overview and Tips to Keep in Mind   91

14. Type 1: Perfectionist – Reformer – Renovator   101

15. Type 2: Nurturer – Helper – Caregiver   109

16. Type 3: Producer – Achiever – Ace   115

17. Type 4: Artist – Individualist – Romantic   123

18. Type 5: Contemplative – Observer – Thinker   129

19. Type 6: Worrier – Skeptic – Doubter   135

20. Type 7: Adventurer – Bon Vivant – Zealot   143

21. Type 8: Leader – Authority – Director   149

22. Type 9: Peacemaker – Diplomat – Mediator   157

23. The Option to Go Deeper   163

Part Three: Plot, Scene, and Emotion

24. Conflict, Plot, and Scene   169

25. Emotional Impact   191

26. Helpful Books, Links, and References   211

About the Author   225

Thanks to all my friends at Vermont College of Fine Arts.

". . . your fiction can be only as successful as the characters who move it and move within it."

Janet Burroway

1.

Creating Characters

AS WRITERS OF FICTION, we have godlike power. We create worlds and populate them with beings. It's a delicious feeling when we've done it successfully. *Successfully*, of course, is the key word.

Each week *Publishers Weekly* magazine distributes several pages of well-respected book reviews on newly released books of all types. Here are some comments culled from recent reviews of fiction.

"unsympathetic characters and lack of action"

"major characters seriously underdeveloped"

"the characters are two-dimensional and predictable to the point of banality."

"it suffers from an unlikable protagonist . . . underdeveloped characters will prevent many readers from ever fully engaging with the protagonist and her struggle."

"Many of the characters are unlikable, which prevents readers from engaging with the story, and stilted dialog . . . hampers what could have been an interesting journey."

"failing to give readers a reason to care about [the protagonist]"

"thinly sketched characters"

"a cartoonish villain"

"one-dimensional villain"

Ouch. But obviously the authors of these poorly reviewed novels thought their writing hit the mark or they wouldn't have published. So how do you know when your characters are well-drawn? How can you avoid getting reviews like these?

I can't guarantee you good reviews. I also can't guarantee that everyone will like your characters, even if they're well-written. But I can show you a way to create deep, believable characters that readers will care about.

When I first began writing novels, I thought all I needed character-wise was basic information – a look, a job, a family, a list of their favorites: music, food, color, pet. It wasn't too hard to arbitrarily assign those traits. But I discovered that, while some of those details were useful, they were shallow. In a nice rejection of my first novel, one editor wrote, "I'm not convinced that your protagonist can carry the weight of this story." She was right. I had not figured out why my main character connected to that particular plot. What made her more worthy of the protagonist role than any other similar character? What made her special?

Shallow characters with superficial traits don't entice readers to identify with them or stick with them through a novel-length story. Speaking from a reader's viewpoint, author Janet Burroway says, "[W]e must find [characters] interesting, we must find them believable, and we must care about what happens to them." As writers, those are our marching orders. We need to create well-rounded characters to engage our readers, who include agents, editors, and reviewers.

But readers aren't the only ones who benefit from believable characters. We writers do too. Superficial traits are not much help when it comes to creating plot and scene, but complex, believable characters pave the way for believable plots. That's because plot is built around how characters act and react in different situations – and *why*. Both the *how* and the *why* require depth. We have to know our characters' desires, fears, beliefs, and motivations, the deep traits that make our imaginary people so believable that readers can identify with our fictional characters as if they were real flesh and blood.

As you know, books on character creation and character-driven plots are not in short supply. So why should I add to that supply? Only because I think I have something to bring to the table: a way of looking at character that may help you. I'm confident that at the least, I can add to the options in your writing toolbox. To do that, I've divided this book into three short sections.

In **Part One** I offer my take on the ages and stages of human development, because part of creating believable characters is making them act their age. We'll look briefly at the emotional, mental, moral, and spiritual norms of each stage. Of course, you may choose to make characters act older or younger than their age, but knowing general stages of human development will allow you to be intentional about your choices.

In **Part Two**, I show you how to dig deeply into your characters' psyches. You've probably seen a variety of models that detail personality types. My favorite is the Enneagram (any-a-gram). *Ennea* means *nine* and indicates that this model describes nine major personality types. The model is usually presented as a geometric figure in which the sections are interconnected. Rooted in the ancient spiritual wisdom of a 4th century mystic from Alexandria, Egypt, the Enneagram has developed over the centuries into today's model. Whether or not it's useful for assessing real life personalities is not for me to say. What I can say is that it can help writers create characters and plots.

When I discovered the Enneagram, I was writing high fantasy, the Angelaeon Circle series, which is an epic story with a large cast. The more I studied the nine-type model, the more I began to see my characters reflected in it. Their personalities began to solidify. I also saw that each character would naturally have certain weaknesses and strengths specific to his or her type. My characters' deep beliefs, desires, fears, and motivations were no longer simply arbitrary guesswork on my part but were linked logically to personality. I could see my main character's immaturities as she began her journey through the story, and I could also see exactly how she would need to change and grow throughout the novels in order to reach a more mature place by the end.

Using the Enneagram helped me avoid stereotyping and instead ensured that my characters would be multi-dimensional. I discovered believable backstory and was able to give my characters credible emotions. Author Renee Swindle says, "Instead of labeling your characters as good or bad or whatever, consider remaining curious. Even if a certain character's backstory doesn't make it into the novel, you should know why and how they became who they are. If you write your so-called 'bad' characters with no sense of insight, or compassion for that matter, you just might end up writing them as flat."

When characters are multi-dimensional, their motives believably fuel conflict, tension, and plot. If you're an experienced writer, the Enneagram may provide a fresh way to deepen and enliven your characters and refresh your view of plot. If you're fairly new to writing, the Enneagram may give you a handle on not only how to create character but also how to use what you know about your character's personality to help build your entire story from scratch.

If you're like me, as you go through the Enneagram, you'll naturally see yourself and your friends (or enemies) described in the nine types. While the Enneagram is usually meant to help self-understanding and self-development, it is not used in academic psychology but in spiritual psychology. If you want to look further into the Enneagram, there are several online sites that can help you. I've listed a couple of resources in the last chapter. Some include a test to guide you toward discovering your own type.

Part Three looks at plot, scene, and emotions. We'll find out how your fully fleshed out characters can drive plot and scene. We'll also explore ways to use your character's type to make his or her emotional responses realistic so that the emotions will resonate with the reader.

Award-winning writer Marion Dane Bauer says that to write what's most universal, we must write what's most personal, which means we must get inside our main characters. This book is intended to help you do exactly that.

Part One

Making Characters Act Their Age

2.

A Brief Overview

YOU CAN USE THIS ages-and-stages section in one of two ways: Read only the stages your characters are in. Or read through all the stages. I recommend the read-through. Here's why:

1. As a writer and inventor of characters, you owe it to yourself to understand a bit about human development. That general knowledge will expand your vision and inform your writing.

2. No matter what age you've made your characters – kindergartner, teen, middle aged, older adult – each of them has a past and a future. Well-developed characters reflect real life. They came from somewhere and are headed somewhere and think of themselves in those terms. You should too.

3. Contemplating a character's past will help you create his backstory. Pondering his future will help you see around

the corner and have a general sense of what's in store for him, age-wise.

4. Seeing the big picture of human development will help you visualize your characters as whole, well-rounded people, which will help you make them believable to your readers.

Several years ago I read a literary novel by a well-known author. Although it was a novel for adults, one of the point of view characters was a ten-year-old girl. But her thoughts and actions felt much older than a ten-year-old. Every time she was in a scene, the discrepancy threw me out of the story, and I had a hard time finishing the book. Of course, you may choose to make a child character precocious or an adult character childish. But that decision should be intentional, based on the normal characteristics of that age group. When it's intentional, you can let the reader know by making it part of the story. Then you can take full advantage of the character not exhibiting the usual traits for her age.

Author Anne Ursu (@anneursu) recently tweeted: "Pet peeve: kids books where the protag is perfectly able to get and articulate her emotions. Why does she need to live through a book then?" Anne is talking about character arc and growth, but I think there's another issue at work as well. While those books are written from the point of view of a child or teen, most of them are filtered through the fingers of adult writers. If those writers are not careful, their characters can easily fall into ways of thinking, speaking, and acting that are out of sync with their age.

Researchers of human development have published various theories and models for the stages we humans typically go through. Dr. Malcolm Watson, a Professor of Psychology at Brandeis University advises, "[E]ach theory must be used with a view of the context in which it was developed and the purpose for which it was developed." Since my purpose is to help you create story characters that range from the youngest to the oldest, I'm using Erik Erikson's model as a framework, adding specific age ranges as general guidelines.

Erikson's theories are especially useful for writers, because he focuses on the development of identity and the particular issues we confront at each stage of our lives. These stages correspond with what I've experienced as a teacher and parent as well as in my own stages of life. Another benefit of Erikson's model is that it easily expands to encompass the spiritual, an aspect that is often ignored or short-changed in our characters. Not that I'm prodding you to emphasize spirituality, but whether our characters are atheists or mystics or adherents to a traditional religious creed, what they choose to believe spiritually becomes part of who they are and influences the decisions they make.

According to Erikson, as our skills, opportunities, relationships, and obligations expand with each stage of our development, we face stage-specific issues or problems critical to establishing our identity, to becoming who we are

– and how we are – as individuals. These issues and problems throw life out of balance and become "crises" as we react emotionally, trying to resolve those issues and put life back into balance. This is exactly what happens in character-driven novels. Life is tipped out balance for the protagonist, and the story centers on getting life back into balance again. Since conflict is at the center of a good story, being aware of these stages and their specific issues can help us create a conflicted character – in other words, a realistic, believable character.

For example, the "crisis" Erikson describes in infancy revolves around whether or not the infant develops trust. This is one of the central issues that permeates an infant's life, day in and day out. If the infant grows to trust his caregivers, then he achieves the overriding emotional task of this stage, and the results are positive. If the task is not achieved, the results are negative, in this case mistrust. So the conflict at this stage is trust vs. mistrust.

I picture the conflict in each stage as a scale, positive on one side, negative on the other. Of course, rarely is life all positive or all negative. During each stage, the scale tips back and forth, depending on the many factors involved. Parents, caregivers, education, social structure, all contribute to positive or negative experiences. Are you beginning to sense story here?

These positive and negative experiences accumulate so that by the time the person grows out of a stage, we can ask:

which direction does his scale tip? If it's weighted toward the positive, then the person emerges from the stage with what Erikson called a strength. Forming strengths is one foundation of a healthy life. In infancy, for example, when the scale is tipped in favor of trust, the strength that results is hope.

But, you may ask, don't people of all ages deal with issues of trust and mistrust? Yes, but the trust/mistrust challenge comes into critical focus in infancy, even though an event later in life can cause the trust issue to rise to the surface again, particularly if mistrust developed in infancy.

Because our characters' choices are often moral, whether we frame them that way or not, within the description of each stage, I include an overview of the stages of moral development described by psychologists Lawrence Kohlberg, Martin Hoffman, and John C. Gibbs. I also look briefly at mental and spiritual growth. For simplicity, I place all of these within the framework of Erikson's stages.

Keep in mind: Any model of development is meant to show human growth in general. Some people enter a stage earlier than usual, others later. You can see, as a writer, how this could also add tension to plot or provide motive if caregivers and peers see the child as weird or abnormal because she was a late-bloomer or a prodigy.

That's another benefit of knowing the basic stages of human development: it gives you insight into backstory, allowing you to see when and why your characters developed their fears and flaws. That, in turn, helps you discover motivations for choices they make in your plot. We'll go deeper into backstory in Part Two and plot in Part Three. The following stages will lay the foundation.

3.

Infants: Birth to Two

TRUST VS. MISTRUST

Emotionally

WE PROBABLY CHANGE more during our first two years than at any other time of life. An infant goes from lying prone to turning over to sitting up; from drinking only liquid to eating solid food; from cooing to babbling to speaking understandable words. But one task underlies all these changes. It's the one I used as an example in the previous chapter: *Trust*. The challenge for the infant is to learn to trust.

So how does that happen? It's really very simple. The infant's caregivers consistently respond to her and take care of her needs. At first she's completely dependent on others for care. So the way her world's interacts with her communicates whether or not she can trust. When she's hungry, is she fed? When she's cold, does someone wrap a blanket or sweater around her? When her diaper is wet, is she given a clean, dry one? As I said earlier, if the scale is tipped in favor of the positive, *trust*, then the strength of *hope* emerges at this stage.

Hope is the belief that life will get better and all will be well. If a child is consistently cared for – fed, cleaned, clothed, held, and loved – then she can be fairly certain that even in moments when she's cold, hungry, wet, uncomfortable, or even hurting, someone will take care of her. She can assume that she'll get what she needs, and everything will turn out all right. So she has hope.

Of course, if the infant is neglected or abused, she learns just the opposite. Maybe she was abandoned. Or due to war or famine or other disasters, she was left needy. Or her caregivers were constantly changing. In such cases, a child learns that she can't trust anyone to take care of her. She distrusts people, believes they are unreliable, and sees the world as unpredictable. As a result, she moves into the next stage with a foundation that is cracked. Instead of carrying a strength with her, she carries a weakness: insecurity – and at the extreme, hopelessness.

Mentally

We're born with certain built-in capabilities like creativity, temperament, curiosity, and the drive to communicate. So learning comes naturally, and mental growth begins immediately. Everything is new. Every interaction is a discovery.

An infant experiences her world in the present moment, in the now, and her "classroom" is the tangible, sensory environment right in front of her, what she can see, hear, smell, touch, and taste at any given moment. The researcher Piaget called this a "sensorimotor" stage, which simply means that infants use their developing motor skills to explore and discover the world around them.

Morally

Infants are born completely egocentric, which is the lowest stage of morality. That does not mean they're making poor moral choices; it simply means they're not making conscious moral choices at all. According to Piaget, they are in a premoral stage. They express their own wants and needs, demanding attention without regard for the wants and needs of others (like Mom, who needs a good night of sleep). But that's because infants are not yet capable of seeing the world from anyone else's perspective, so they don't understand that other people have needs too. In fact, at first an infant seems to consider her primary caregiver to be an extension of herself.

Still, the stepping stones of moral thinking are being laid even in infancy, first with the basic feelings of comfort and discomfort, pleasure and pain. Even more important is the awareness of a caregiver's acceptance or rejection. Because respect for others is the foundation of morality, when an infant feels accepted and respected, she is on the way to accepting and respecting others. Conversely, when an infant feels rejected, she is on the way to rejecting others.

The goal of moral development is empathy, according to theorist Martin Hoffman. But empathy is slow to develop. We may think that a newborn has an innate sense of empathy, because she cries when she hears other babies cry. The truth is, her response is egocentric. She is not empathizing with the other babies but cries simply because hearing them cry makes her feel distressed. Even a six-month-old faced with a distressed person will try to comfort *herself* by sucking her thumb or clinging to her mother or asking to be picked up. By the time she's one year old, she will try to comfort the distressed person. But why? Because the other person is upsetting *her*.

One basic requirement for the growth of morality is understanding cause and effect. We have to know that what we say and do has consequences that affect other people.

Infants are learning that they can cause certain effects. They can evoke smiles and frowns, and they quickly learn to understand "yes" and "no." They're also sensitive to their caregiver's tone of voice and body language, both of which indicate approval and disapproval. Infants depend on these outward cues of the cause and effect to guide them toward right choices. But moral development is a process, and children don't correctly discern between right and wrong *consistently* until they're about six years old.

SPIRITUALLY

James Fowler, a researcher who authored a classic study of faith development, labeled infancy as a stage of "undifferentiated faith," which means that the beginnings of spiritual sensitivity (trust, courage, hope, love) are not experienced as separate and distinct but are lumped into one feeling: good. In simple terms, the infant begins to feel a very basic sense of good and bad, pain and pleasure, trust and mistrust.

At this point, these feelings are not attached to any idea of the divine. Instead the infant sees them as part of the physical, sensory world of her experience. She does not know the words *God* or *care* or *love*, and in fact cannot know them in the abstract. But she does know the feeling of being loved and cared for. Or she feels the lack of care and love. That's the thing about the spiritual: It's not neutral. If you don't have care and love, you miss it. It becomes an emptiness. A lack. A need.

Remember Erikson's description of this stage's conflict? Trust vs. mistrust. Fowler says, "The strength of trust, autonomy, hope and courage (or their opposites) developed in this phase underlie (or threaten to undermine) all that comes later in faith development." This applies to any faith or religion, any higher power the child might be taught to honor and place her hope and trust in.

When You Write

You can use this basic information not only to craft believable babies and caregivers but also to create believable backstory for any of your characters. You can find pointers in this section that will lead you to understand where a character's innate sense of trust came from or where her strength of hope originated. On the other hand, maybe this is where her distrust and loss of hope started. That's not to say that distrust and loss of hope can't develop later. It can creep in at any later stage, piggybacking on other negatives. But if your character later loses hope, at least her earliest memories might include the assurance that "once upon a time, I trusted people and I had hope."

BIRTH TO TWO

- egocentric
- premoral
- undifferentiated faith
- sensorimotor interaction with the world

CONFLICT: TRUST VS. MISTRUST

STRENGTH: HOPE

4.

Early Childhood: Two and Three

AUTONOMY VS. SHAME

Emotionally

ACCORDING TO ERIKSON, two- and three-year-old children develop either *autonomy* or *shame*. An autonomous person is one who rules himself, which is exactly what two- and three-year-olds seem to want. They are beginning the process of becoming independent from their caregivers in order to establish their own unique identities. Of course, the search for identity can be a lifelong pursuit, but this is where it begins.

If you've ever been around a two- or three-year-old, you know that they exert their autonomy and want to do things for themselves. Caregivers who realize that this is normal and beneficial will encourage their toddler to take on age appropriate tasks like brushing his teeth, washing his face, and picking up toys. As the child learns to be independent in these small ways, he develops a sense of autonomy.

Of course, there are many things a young child is not capable of doing – and many things he is not allowed to do. So the key to whether or not a child develops a sense of autonomy is the attitude of the caregiver. When the child needs help, does the caregiver step in with criticism and condemnation or with encouragement and pride at the child's attempts? If a child is not allowed to do simple tasks that he is perfectly capable of doing – or if his attempts are met with constant criticism and judgment – he develops a sense of shame. According to Erikson, shame is a feeling of being exposed. In this case, the child feels that what has been exposed is his own deficiency and inadequacy.

If the scale is tipped in favor of autonomy, then the child leaves this stage with a strength that Erikson calls *will*, which is an appropriate description of twos and threes. We often call them strong-willed. And while we may moan about how difficult it is to go head to head with a two-year-old, in a few years that child may need the strength of will to stand up to peer pressure. To develop our identities, we have to develop our wills, and this stage is where will stakes its claim in no uncertain terms.

MENTALLY

Early childhood begins what Piaget called the "preoperational" stage, which lasts until the child is about seven years old. While some experts believe that Piaget's stages are too rigid, for our purposes, they're workable. *Operation* is Piaget's way of describing a thought process that allows a child "to do in his mind what before was done physically." Adult-like, logical reasoning is operational. So *preoperational* means that at this stage, a child is not able to reason with adult-like logic.

But that doesn't mean young children aren't logical. It simply means that they think with childlike logic. One three-year-old exclaimed, "Mommy, I know why they call it the moon! Because the cow jumped over it and said, MOOO!" Young children also tend to think literally. (Mom lost her voice – where did she lose it? Maybe I can find it for her.) And young children don't understand the flow of time. "A long time ago" was yesterday's at Grandma's house. If you tell a young child, "Your birthday is only two weeks away," he may wake up tomorrow morning and ask, "Is it my birthday yet?"

Twos and threes still see themselves as the center of their universe as they try to make sense of the outside world that revolves around them and their everyday activities. They move through their world like a whirlwind, constantly learning through their five senses. To find out how they affect the world, they perform simple cause and effect experiments: What will happen if I push this button, pull this string, or take that apart? All this exploring keeps their caregivers hopping.

MORALLY

As Erikson pointed out, *will* is the strength that should develop at this stage. That's both good news and challenging news. Good news because it's a sign that the child is maturing. Challenging news because it means the child is now aware that he can make deliberate choices. With deliberate choices come moral choices: Do I assert my will or submit my will? Everyone in the child's world is drawn into his struggle to find the balance.

For toddlers the struggle with will is intensely difficult. Even though they're maturing, they're still quite egocentric, so everything they see, smell, taste, touch or hear is "mine." When they're about eighteen months old, they start to understand that other people have feelings and needs too, but throughout early childhood, they will still have a hard time acknowledging the difference between "mine" and "yours."

Even the play of young children reflects this struggle. Twos and threes engage in what's called "parallel play," which means they play side by side but not cooperatively together. The good news is that as children near age three, they reach a developmental milestone: They begin "perspective taking." That means the toddler begins to be able to understand another person's viewpoint and realize that other people have rights, opinions, possessions, and feelings just the way he does.

One two-year-old girl, who was not yet at the perspective-taking stage, hit a little boy in her play group. Her mother confronted her, appalled, asking, "How do you think that felt?" The little girl studied her fist and answered, "It felt pretty good." She interpreted even Mom's question egocentrically.

Dr. Thomas Lickona, who has studied developing morality, has a wonderfully concise way of explaining these stages: "What's right" to a child at this stage, he says, is "to get my own way." This is stage one of morality, according to researchers. It's what we might call "superficial" morality, in which the reason to be "good" is to gain reward and/or avoid punishment. (Some older kids and even adults revert to – or live in – this immature stage.)

With superficial morality, children depend on consistently enforced rules to help them discern what's right and what's wrong. Consistent rules also give children a sense of safety and security. They may buck the rules, but having no rules, or rules that are inadequate or inconsistently enforced, leaves children feeling uncertain, insecure, and anxious.

One thing about toddlers: They usually have to be told the same rules over and over again. It's hard for them to generalize and understand that a rule may apply everywhere and in all situations. In other words, if a child is told to share at Timmy's house, he takes that directive as specific and limited, not as a general "always share your toys" rule. So with a change of playmate or location, he may have to hear the directive again.

SPIRITUALLY

If children are taught to believe in God, this is the stage when they begin to form ideas and images of what God is like. Often these images have human characteristics. I call this the "fantasy/imitative" stage, based on Fowler's description of this stage as "the fantasy-filled, imitative phase in which the child can be powerfully and permanently influenced by examples, moods, actions and stories" of the significant adults in his life. This stage of faith lasts until the child is about six or seven.

Fowler emphasizes the adult's tremendous responsibility at this stage. He says, "The imagination and fantasy life of a child can be exploited by witting or unwitting adults." Religious stories, images, and symbols that adults share with children "can prove life-opening and sustaining of love, faith and courage," or they can give rise "to fear, rigidity and the brutalization of souls." That's because young children generally believe what they are told without questioning whether or not it's true. If they're told there's a Santa Claus or an Easter bunny or a tooth fairy, they believe it, because they still have difficulty distinguishing between fantasy and reality, so imagination plays a big role in their lives.

Think of all the religious stories and concepts young children are taught. They don't question or weigh what's true or untrue but believe what they're told, just as they believe in Santa Claus. They assume that adults are telling the truth, which means that young children have a taken-for-granted faith.

That's the "fantasy" related part of this stage. What about the "imitative"? Young children cannot enter the adult world, so they imitate significant adults, mimicking what they've witnessed of the outward expressions of adult faith – religious forms, practices, rites, and rituals.

S<small>IGNIFICANT</small> A<small>DULTS</small>

I want to pause here for a more focused look at the term *significant adult*, because I'll refer to it again in the following stages, and it can be a source of fuel for your writing. The significant adult is the person whose influence on the child affects the child's choices, which in turn affects his future path. So for any given child, we can ask, "Who are the significant adults in his life?" The obvious traditional answer is "Mom and Dad." But that's not always the case in real life, and it's even rarer in fiction. It's true that parents will always have a significant impact on their children, even if one or both parents are missing. So, yes, the absence of a parent is very significant. But when I use the term *significant adult*, I'm referring to adults who are present in the child's life, playing an active role, and having a strong influence on the child's choices and values.

The significant adult provides a moral compass for the child. Novelist Scott Spencer, in a radio interview, spoke about the importance of a moral compass, asking, "What do you do when you are physically away from your moorings?" (A question that propelled him through his plot.) Of course, the answer is: It depends on your moral compass. The interviewer commented, "People close to us are our memory banks. They help explain our lives to us." In a child's life, these people are the ones I refer to as significant adults.

To find out who the significant people are for a particular child, ask, "Who spends time with the child? (Not just in the same house, but *with* the child.) Who listens to the child? Who plays with the child?" The answer to these questions will usually reveal the identity of the significant people in the child's life. And they may not always be adults.

Note: You can ask these same questions of any character of any age to find out not only who influenced them in the past but also who influences them now.

When You Write

You can use this basic information not only to craft believable toddlers and their caregivers but also to create believable backstory for any of your characters. You can find pointers in this section that can lead you to understand where a character's innate sense of autonomy came from or where his strength of will originated. On the other hand, maybe this is where his shame started. Maybe that's the reason he discounts or subordinates his will. For example, if he brought mistrust from his infancy into this stage, he may not risk attempting the tasks that would lead to autonomy. And if he develops shame at this stage, he may be wary of taking on tasks that would lead to independence in the next stage.

Of course, shame can develop at a later stage if circumstances are traumatic enough. If so, the character might remember a time, early in his life, when he was confident and unafraid to express his will.

TWO AND THREE

- fantasy/reality confusion
- strong imagination
- impressionable, gullible
- imitating significant adults
- childlike logic, literal thinking
- developing a "sense of other"
- rule dependent

CONFLICT: AUTONOMY VS. SHAME

STRENGTH: WILL

Early Childhood: Fours and Fives

INITIATIVE VS. GUILT

Emotionally

THE NEXT LIFE CRISIS, according to Erikson, is the result of the struggle between initiative and guilt. A person with initiative does things without being asked. She's assertive, thinks independently, and is what we would call a self-starter. This is a good description of most four and five year old children. They're little scientists, trying to impose order on their rapidly expanding world. They're out to explore, examine, and discover. Eager to learn and know, they ask hundreds of questions a day, some so off-the-wall that they have no real, logical answer, others quite deep, like my son's "Why does the skin on your body never end?"

When a child's natural inclination to explore is encouraged, she develops a sense of initiative. There are, of course, limits to what the four- or five-year-old is able to do. There are also things she can't be allowed to explore. Even so, initiative can develop if caregivers respond respectfully, affirming her impulse to explore and discover. On the other hand, if the child is ridiculed or continually restricted and told she is not capable, she begins to feel guilty for her natural curiosity and urge to explore.

But if a child develops her sense of initiative, the strength that emerges is called *purpose*. She senses that there's a purpose for her curiosity and questions, a purpose for the order of nature and the world around her, and perhaps most important, a purpose for her in the world.

MENTALLY

Fours and fives are still in the preoperational stage, and they still learn primarily through their five senses. But they're developing significant mental skills. One of the most important of these skills, according to researcher Howard Gardner, is the ability to understand and work with symbols. Fours and fives, just beginning this growth, still often think literally and with childlike logic. One father reported that he and his four-year-old son were walking down a flight of stairs when the boy suddenly stopped and exclaimed, "I know why we have cracks in our bottoms! It's so we can go down the stairs!" Another preschooler saw a house being moved, sitting on the flat bed of a truck. "That house must have been really dirty," he said. "They had to lift it up to sweep all the dirt out from under it." Logical. From a child's point of view.

Fours and fives are proud of their age and may announce it to anyone they meet. They are now aware that they're growing, getting older, better, smarter, and stronger. This focus on age may have to do with their growing interest in numbers and counting. They seem to want to count everything, which ties into their expanding ability to make and use symbols.

Because exploration and discovery are so much a part of their lives, fours and fives are more aware of what's happening in the world around them. By five, they're also beginning to recognize the difference between fantasy and reality. But there's still a lot they don't understand, so they may develop fears they haven't had before. They want and need understanding and comfort. Again, they can easily be made to feel guilty, not only for what they do and say but also for what they want and feel.

Morally

At about age five, children move up to a new level of morality that, according to Dr. Lickona, views "right" as "doing what I'm told." Children of this stage still depend on rules to guide them to know and choose what's right. However, their conscience is beginning to develop as they internalize the teaching and training of earlier years. If they've been taught to respect others, they know it's wrong to take toys from other children, it's right to share, it's wrong to hit, it's right to help, and so on. They have a better understanding of the concept of consequences, if/then, cause and effect.

Dr. Robert Solomon, a professor of philosophy, points out that the conscience is, in many ways, the sensibility of "being caught in the act." In essence, we "catch ourselves." That's what moral education does for us. We learn to control ourselves. "Our own self-consciousness imposes the internal judgment," he says.

Of course, children don't always go by what their developing consciences tell them (and neither do we adults). They share selectively, picking and choosing what to share and when, and they still have trouble seeing from any viewpoint but their own. So they continue to need external help to confirm when they are on the right or wrong track.

The play of fours and fives reflects this new level of morality. Instead of playing "parallel" (side by side but not together) like toddlers do, fours and fives engage in "associative play." They interact cooperatively with other children. "You be the mommy, and I'll be the baby." Or "You be the store man, and I'll come buy some ice cream." Or "You make the road with the blocks, and I'll drive my car over it." This interaction requires a level of respect for the other person that indicates a higher level of morality.

Fours and fives also begin identifying with the values of the significant people in their lives. A five-year-old may report with shock, "Did you hear the word *he* said?!" Or "Do you know what movie *they're* going to watch tonight?!" Four- and five-year olds are discovering that not all people share the same values. As for them? They identify with the values of their significant adults and use those values as a guide in their all-or-nothing thinking. To them there are no moral nuances. Everything is either bad or good, wrong or right, black or white, nothing in between.

SPIRITUALLY

Four- and five-year-olds are still in the fantasy-imitative stage of faith that began around age two. They live what they imagine and imitate the visible signs of faith of their significant adults. As we learned earlier, the young child believes whatever he is told. That's why we often idealize the "pure" faith of a child. His faith is taken for granted, and he does not question it. In other words, "that's just the way it is," and that's perfectly normal for this stage.

WHEN YOU WRITE

You can use this basic information not only to craft believable preschoolers and their caregivers but also to create believable backstory for any of your characters. You can find clues in this section that may help you understand where a character's sense of initiative came from or where her strength of purpose originated. On the other hand, maybe this is where her guilt feelings began. Maybe that's the reason she lacks initiative, direction, and purpose.

Of course, guilt can develop later due to other circumstances. If that happens, she might remember a time, early in her life, when she took initiative and felt that her life had purpose.

> ## Four and Five
>
> - starting to sort out fantasy from reality
> - strong imagination
> - childlike logic, literal thinking
> - good/bad, safe/dangerous
> - rule dependent
> - conscience developing
> - identifying with values of significant adults
>
> Conflict: Initiative vs. Guilt
>
> Strength: Purpose

6.

Six Through Nine

INDUSTRY VS. INFERIORITY

THIS STAGE COVERS a broader age range than the previous stages did, but the youngest and oldest of this group deal with the same positive/negative conflict. Still, a six-year-old is quite different from a nine-year-old, so before we consider the general characteristics of this stage, let's see how the ages normally differ. Chip Wood, a principal and teacher, gives a good in-depth look at specific age differences and needs in his book *Yardsticks*, which I recommend if you want to study this further. The following is only an overview. Remember that these are general characteristics. Temperament, personality, and environment are variables that will factor into the specifics for each individual child.

Six:

- sloppy (Process more important than product.)

- competitive

- eager and enthusiastic

Seven:

- intense and serious

- conscientious

- self-absorbed and self-conscious

Eight:

- speedy, energetic

- full of ideas

- focused on exploring their potential

Nine:

- worried, complaining, negative

- individualistic

- prone to exaggeration

I call this group *collectors*, because they collect things: rocks or baseball cards, stamps or stuffed animals, pennants or coins or model cars. Most of all, they collect friends. They want to be part of the group, to be an accepted member of their community, whether that's their neighborhood, school group, sports team, or club.

Emotionally

Erikson saw this time as a critical stage for creating either a sense of industry or a feeling of inferiority in children. So what is industry? An industrious person is someone who is busy being productive. That's an appropriate description of six- to nine-year-olds, who are mastering new skills and are eager to show their prowess: How fast can I run? How high can I jump? How far can I throw the ball? How many times can I skip rope without missing? How well can I knit or draw or make a bracelet? In a sense, this is another way of collecting, but this time they're collecting kudos, if only in their own minds. When children in this stage are encouraged in their efforts to be busy and productive, and when they discover where they can succeed, they develop a sense of industry.

Inferiority, the negative side of this stage, can develop in a variety of ways. Peers play a greater role now, and because kids want to fit into the group and belong, if they're bullied or rejected, they can easily feel inferior. The adults in a child's life play an important role too. If adults set goals that are too high, and the child can't live up to expectations, he feels inferior. This is especially true if he perceives that love and acceptance are based on his performance and achievements. For that child, the consequences of failure are enormous.

Inferiority can also result if an adult does the child's work for him. Adults know they can do projects faster and better, but when the adult takes over, it signals that "you're not capable; your work is not good enough." Or perhaps the adult doesn't take over, but neither does she allow the child to practice his skills. Every time the child gets out the glue and paint, the adult tells him to "put it away; all you ever do is make a mess." Not that the adult should allow chaos, but as with previous stages, there are respectful ways to respond that will encourage the child and set limits at the same time.

At this stage, children want to know, "What do *I* do well?" Adults can play a key role by pointing out the child's strengths and accomplishments, giving him a vision for who he is and what he can do. When a child goes through this stage developing the positive sense of industry, he reaps a bonus: the strength of *competence* (built on the word *compete*). He feels capable. This powerful asset forms a strong foundation for accomplishments that lie ahead.

MENTALLY

According to Piaget, the six-year-old is in his last year of moving from being pre-operational, reasoning with child-like logic, to being "concrete operational," a new stage that lasts through age eleven. In this stage, the child can reason with adult logic but does this best when he has something concrete on which to base his thinking. In other words, the child needs to see or handle something. It must be physically present or physically represented for him to reason logically about it.

More recent research has shown that in some areas, children reach this concrete operational stage earlier than Piaget thought. Howard Gardner believes a child may be preoperational in the area of language but concrete operational in the area of drawing or number. This would account for why some children seem to understand symbolism, with concrete representations, in certain areas much earlier than age seven. Still, age seven is often known as "the age of reason." By then most children have moved from literal interpretations of words, events, and stories to an understanding of symbolism and deeper meanings.

Children are now able to perceive distance and space more accurately. Because they better understand the flow of time, they begin studying events of history and can perceive them chronologically. They also memorize more easily and are able to retain a lot of information. Age nine is sometimes called "the golden age of memory."

Morally

About age six, children begin to *consistently* discern correctly between right and wrong, although they still depend on rules to guide their behavior. From six to nine, they seem to have a strong, innate sense of justice and are alert to infractions of the rules. "It's not fair" is a common complaint, and they're quick to point a finger at anyone who breaks the rules. At this age, children have a fairness-focused "eye for an eye, tooth for a tooth" sense of morality. But they often have a double standard as well: Justice for all, mercy for me. Dr. Lickona says they believe "right" is to "look out for myself but be fair to those who are fair to me," stage two of morality: "concrete moral reciprocity."

Spiritually

Throughout this stage, children still have a taken-for-granted faith and generally continue to believe what they're taught about religion and spirituality. However, they also begin asking insightful and sometimes uncomfortable questions. One six-year-old asked, "Why is God a He, not a She?"

Fowler calls this the mythic-literal stage, because the child's growing faith – whatever that faith may be – depends in large part on the stories he sees and hears each day, especially stories told by significant adults. Fowler says, "the person begins to take on for him- or herself the stories, beliefs and observances that symbolize belonging to his or her community."

WHEN YOU WRITE

You can use this basic information not only to craft believable six- through nine-year-olds and their caregivers but also to create believable backstory for any of your characters. You can find clues in this section that may help you understand where a character's sense of industry came from or where his strength of competence originated. On the other hand, maybe this is where his feelings of inferiority began. Maybe that's the reason he feels incompetent.

Of course, inferiority can develop later due to life circumstances. If so, he might remember a previous time in his life when he was industrious and felt competent.

SIX THROUGH NINE

- moving from literal to symbolic reasoning
- concrete operational
- competitive
- rule oriented
- story centered faith
- eye for eye morality

CONFLICT: INDUSTRY VS. INFERIORITY

STRENGTH: COMPETENCE

7.

Tweens: Ten Through Twelve

INDUSTRY VS. INFERIORITY
   and
IDENTITY FORMATION
VS. IDENTITY CONFUSION

Tweens are sandwiched in an awkward space between elementary age children and the youth of adolescence. I say awkward, because they have a foot in each world and often seesaw back and forth. Some tweens definitely lean younger, toward childhood. Others already seem to be young teens. But most of them vacillate between child and teen, which is why we'll see some of the previous stage reflected in this chapter as well as previews of the coming adolescent stage.

Advertising and media focus a huge amount of attention on kids this age, because advertisers know that parents spend more on tweens than on any other age group. So kids in this stage are targets. One reason is because they're growing more self-conscious, peer-conscious, and body-conscious. In other words, image-conscious. And that perfectly fits advertisers goals, because they're hired to make consumers believe that purchasing and using certain products will enhance their image.

Another reason advertisers target tweens is because kids at this stage are moving rapidly toward the adolescent's desire to develop her personal identity, to decide who she is or at least how she would like to be perceived. Product creators, sellers, and advertisers want their products and brands to become part of the young person's identity: "I'm a Pepsi guy." "I'm a (fill-in-the-blank with the popular clothing brand) kind of girl." The product-peddlers want to get a head start on claiming loyalty, so this age looks like their perfect match.

As with the previous stage, there's a lot of differences between the younger and older ends of the tween group. Again, Chip Wood in *Yardsticks* provides a good look at each specific age. Here's an overview:

TEN:

- relatively calm, cooperative, content

- quick to anger but quick to forgive

ELEVEN:

- argumentative

- moody and sensitive

- self-absorbed

TWELVE:

- more reasonable

- more self-aware

- energetic and enthusiastic

The biggest leap probably occurs between ten and eleven, which seems to be a transition period. Parents usually experience this transition as a decrease in communication. The door to the tween's bedroom, which was always open before, is now closed and may have a sign on it: "Private." Or "Knock Before Entering." Or even "Keep Out." In general, boys become more restless, and girls become moody. Many girls begin menstruating, although the average age for this is twelve and a half. The point is, tweens are moving into the world of emotional weather patterns we might call "hormonal disturbances." They're thrown out of balance, uncertain, and often uncomfortable with the changes they're experiencing.

Another factor that makes this stage awkward is that boys usually enter puberty later than girls. Of course, puberty comes later for some girls as well. Social groupings tend to mirror this uneven rate of maturity. In previous stages, boys and girls generally mixed spontaneously during activities, but now they tend to gather in separate groups. And among those of the same gender, those who mature earlier often flock together in cliques, leaving late-bloomers to form separate social groups.

EMOTIONALLY

As in the previous stage, tweens have the task of continuing to develop a sense of *industry*, but now we can add the task of *identity formation*. As we saw in the previous chapter, developing a sense of industry involves the child mastering skills and discovering abilities. This discovery becomes a foundation for the tween's growing search for identity, which will continue through the teen years.

The negative side of the equation is the sense of *inferiority* we discussed in connection with the previous stage. Add the growing self-consciousness of the tween, and we get the beginnings of teen angst: What do *they* think of me? Still, tweens don't usually spend an inordinate amount of time in self-reflection, not like they will in the next stage.

The negative of identity formation is *identity confusion*, which we'll discuss in more detail in the following chapter. For now, we can note that if a tween is developing a sense of industry and identity, the strength of *competence* should continue to emerge, and the strength of *fidelity* should begin developing. Since adolescence is the time in which the process of identity and fidelity formation reaches its peak, we'll save that discussion for the following chapter as well.

Mentally

The tween stage is the second fastest period of brain growth, infancy to age five being the fastest. The passage from childhood into adolescence marks the transition into the stage Piaget calls "formal operational," which starts around age twelve. With formal operations, teens begin to be able to reason with adult logic. Again, we'll take a deeper look in the next chapter. But one of the welcome benefits of this brain growth is that tweens are beginning to be able to concentrate for longer stretches of time.

And there's more good news: This brain growth signals a coming maturity that will bring the ability to process reality maturely. The bad news is that it doesn't happen overnight but develops slowly over a fairly long period of time. Psychologist Daniel Goleman says, "The prefrontal-limbic neural circuitry crucial to the acquisition of social and emotional abilities is the last part of the human brain to become anatomically mature, a developmental task not completed until the mid-twenties." So the tween stage is the beginning of a long haul.

When we looked at early childhood, we noted that children are not able to consistently tell the difference between fantasy and reality until they're about five years old. But there is a type of fantasy, "wishful thinking," that continues through the tween and even teen years. It goes something like this: "Me? I can drink beer and not get drunk." Or "I won't get pregnant." Or "I won't get an STD." "Those things may happen to other people, but not to me." Daniel J. Siegel, in *Brainstorm: The Power and the Purpose of the Teen Brain*, puts a little different slant on it. He says most teens are aware of the risks but often decide that the risks are worth the reward. For girls, this stage lasts until around the age of sixteen or seventeen. For boys, it lasts into their early twenties. So here again, when we discuss tweens, we find ourselves flowing right into the next stage.

Morally

Tweens still have the rule-oriented, fairness-focused, double standard morality that characterizes younger kids, but they are shifting from Concrete Reciprocity (I'll be fair to whoever's fair to me) to Ideal Reciprocity (basically the Golden Rule: treat others the way you want to be treated). "Right," says Dr. Lickona, is generally considered "being nice so that others will think well of me and I can think well of myself." Tweens still tend to reason with payback logic – getting even, balancing the score. But because of their maturing mental capacities, they're getting better at thinking through social issues and suggesting solutions. They can also do a better job of gauging right and wrong.

On the other hand, tweens tend to be relationally shallow and self-serving. They may act or speak impulsively, not thinking about the consequences. As they grow through this stage, they often test limits and challenge boundaries that seem arbitrary to them. And their dilemmas become increasingly more teenlike. The biggest influences on their values are media, peers, school, and parents, and they tend to conform to the wishes of the significant people in their lives, the people who spend time with them, work and play with them, and really listen to them when they have something to say.

SPIRITUALLY

Tweens still have the story-centered faith of the previous stage. This includes the faith-related or spiritually significant stories told by their parents, their faith community, and their friends. It also includes their own personal stories as they experience – or don't experience – a connection with the spiritual.

Another cultural factor is pluralism. A pluralistic society is one in which each different ethnic, racial, religious, and social group keeps its own identity and culture within a common civilization. Our society is pluralistic, which means that tweens will compare their spiritual beliefs with the beliefs of others. They may begin questioning, challenging, perhaps even arguing with the beliefs they have been taught, beliefs that until now, they have taken for granted. As they mature, they become more sensitive to inconsistencies between what they've been taught and what they actually see and hear from the significant adults in their lives.

When You Write

You can use this basic information not only to craft believable tweens but also to create believable backstory for any of your characters. You can find clues in this section that may help you understand where a character's strong sense of industry and identity came from or where her strength of competence and fidelity originated. On the other hand, maybe this is where her feelings of inferiority began or why she is seems emotionally lost, still searching for her identity.

Of course, life circumstances can always shake us up and send us back to questioning who we are, but if we've developed a strong sense of self in the tween and teen years, we're on more solid ground when that happens. If that's the case with your character, she might remember a previous time in her life when she felt industrious and confident about her identity.

TEN THROUGH TWELVE

- one foot in childhood, one in adolescence
- rule oriented, fairness focused
- challenge boundaries
- story centered faith, questioning
- self-conscious, image-conscious
- peer and gender sensitive, forming groups

CONFLICT: INDUSTRY VS. INFERIORITY AND IDENTITY FORMATION VS. IDENTITY CONFUSION

STRENGTH: COMPETENCE AND THE BEGINNING OF FIDELITY

8.

Adolescence: Thirteen To Twenty

IDENTITY FORMATION VS. IDENTITY CONFUSION

THE BOUNDARIES BETWEEN all stages are fluid, a fact that's reflected by the recommended age categories in publishers' book lists. The *Publishers Weekly* review section always shows varying age ranges for MG (Middle Grade) and YA (Young Adult). A recent issue shows one publisher listing MG books with the age range of 7-10, while another recommends 8-12. Agent and author Marie Lamba defines YA as a category for ages thirteen through eighteen, but publishers list some YA books for ages 9-12, others for 10-14, and still others for 12 and up. Sometimes these divisions are called "young YA" or "low YA" and "older YA." Then there's the fairly new category designated New Adult (NA) for the college/early career stage.

Obviously the boundaries are not rigid. The main thing to remember when creating a character is that the overview of human development is meant to be simply a framework to guide your creative decisions. So while some researchers now consider adolescence to continue into the early twenties, I'm categorizing it as thirteen to twenty.

As in the previous stages, there's a great difference between the youngest and oldest in this category. Chip Wood's *Yardsticks* can give you a deeper look, but here's a general list of traits to be aware of:

Thirteen:

- Boys lag behind girls about a year in signs of physical maturity.

- Peer pressure increases.

- They can be touchy, withdrawn, sarcastic, worried about schoolwork.

Fourteen:

- Boys generally enter puberty.

- Their identity tends to be wrapped up in the peer group.

- They distance themselves from adults.

FIFTEEN:

- Their desire is to be accepted.

- They are establishing their own value system.

- They want to do things their way.

- They may argue for argument's sake.

SIXTEEN:

- They tend to be idealistic and may become disillusioned.

- They are more individual-focused and less group-focused.

- They show strong convictions, strongly expressed.

SEVENTEEN TO TWENTY:

- They embody both a sophisticated adult and a sensitive youth.

- Both sexes are physically mature and interested in each other.

EMOTIONALLY

Teens, as they mature year by year, leave the awkwardness of the tween stage and gradually become young men and women. Young adults. This is the last stage of what began in infancy: becoming an independent individual. It's no surprise, then, that the adolescent's main task is to develop a sense of *identity*. What began in the previous stage now intensifies as the teen tries to figure out who he is, what he believes, and where he plans to go. He explores different roles available to him and chooses a path to pursue for the future.

For this reason, adolescents continue to be targets for the marketing pitches of almost anyone and everyone who has a product to sell. According to the documentary "Merchants of Cool," in 2008 teens were "a market segment worth an estimated $150 billion a year." In an in-depth look at marketing and the youth culture, commentator David Kupelian said that "teenagers increasingly look to the media to provide them with a ready-made identity predicated on today's version of what's cool." But, he pointed out, advertising and media are interested in promoting a *consumer* identity, not necessarily a *healthy* identity.

In fact, part of the teen struggle centers on just exactly what identity is and where to find it, because what's being sold as identity is really about *image*. True identity is based on *character* in the sense of personal integrity. Beliefs. Values. So in the identity search, teens often try ideas on for size. This sometimes leads them to express themselves very strongly on issues in order to hear themselves take a stand that differs from the views of the adult(s) in the discussion. In essence, the teen is trying to prove what the two-year-old discovered so long ago: I am a person in my own right. I am not you.

Social media is another place teens try to establish their identity and exhibit their image. Anastasia Goodstein of Ypulse, an online site that covers youth marketing and research, said of social media, "Teens are narcissistic and exhibitionist. For teens, especially, who are going through this stage where they're constantly looking for that affirmation and validation and response for everything they are, it's addictive." Media and advertising fit right in, since, "Brands are about giving you value, giving you self-esteem," says Juliet Schor in her book *Born to Buy*. Peggy Orenstein, in *Cinderella Ate My Daughter*, says that the "all-pervasive media machine aimed at our daughters . . . tells them that how you look *is* how you feel, as well as who you are." That's not good news, but it's the way our world works right now. Image, identity, and marketing are all connected in the teen world.

Teens push against boundaries, and adults usually push back. Ideally as teens move through this stage, adults allow them to make more and more of their own decisions. With loving support and age-appropriate boundaries, teens are usually able to begin figuring out who they are and what they stand for. On the other hand, if a teen is still treated like a child, or if his views and opinions are not heard or valued, or if someone maps out his future path for him, he may develop a sense of *identity confusion*.

But if the scale is tipped in favor of the positive, and the teen is growing into his own sense of identity, he emerges from this stage with the strength of *fidelity*, which means *faithfulness*. In this case, fidelity simply means being faithful to his beliefs and values. Being true to who he is.

MENTALLY

By now, the adolescent is definitely in the formal operational stage. That means he can think about thinking, which is something he couldn't do previously. He is also growing more adept at using adult logic and dealing with abstract concepts and hypothetical situations. However, many teens choose *not* to reason more maturely or use mature thinking sporadically, says Kevin Huggins, who has spent years working with youth. But why would a teen choose not to think maturely?

- Teens may reason immaturely if they're under a lot of stress. When we're stressed, we tend to revert to more immature ways of thinking and acting. (That applies to anyone of any age. More specifics on this in Part Two.) There's a great list of the top 40 stressors for teens in *The Power to Prevent Suicide: A Guide for Teens Helping Teens* by Nelson, Galas, and Cobain. Their list ranges from major events (a parent dies or parents divorce) to more minor issues (get a job, go to summer camp). I've found this list very helpful when I'm looking for curveballs to throw at my teen characters.

- Teens may reason immaturely, because mature thinking grows out of pain, problems, and hardship, exactly what they – and we – try to avoid. Parents contribute to immaturity by being overprotective and over-controlling as they try to save their kids from . . . yes, pain, problems, and hardship. (Writers often do this too – with their characters.)

- Teens may reason immaturely, because mature thinking develops by interacting with people who think maturely, specifically older, wiser adults. Many young people spend most of their time with peers and very little time with mature adults. Being part of a peer group is appealing, because it confers teens with an automatic identity. But it also comes with a risk if they decide not to go along with the group-think. They may have a hard time asserting their individual identity.

As a teen's horizons broaden each year, he sees a wider range of choices than he saw before. He also begins to realize that each choice comes with corresponding risks and rewards. What to do? Decision-making may become difficult, and a teen may be slow to actually make a choice, whether it's mundane, like what to order at the food court, or critical, like whether or not to sleep with his girlfriend. So while teens can be impulsive, they can also be indecisive, anxiously worrying and weighing their choices.

Another characteristic of teens is their tendency to exaggerate and respond with over-the-top reactions. And they often contradict themselves. One moment a sixteen-year-old girl proclaims, "I can't stand chocolate." A short time later, she's saying, "Snickers! That's my favorite candy!"

MORALLY

Novelist Orson Scott Card wrote that the life of the adolescent is "full of passion, intensity, magic, and infinite possibility; but lacking responsibility, rarely expecting to have to stay and bear the consequences of error. Everything is played at twice the speed and twice the volume in the adolescent – the romantic – life." That's a reminder of the "wishful thinking" type of fantasy that characterizes this stage, the "it won't happen to me" mindset. As I mentioned previously, that type of wishful thinking lasts until around sixteen or seventeen for girls and into the early twenties for boys.

As a result of formal reasoning, an adolescent can think about what others might be thinking of him. He may also contemplate how different value systems would work in his life as he looks for what "fits" him, which means he may set aside his parents' viewpoint, at least for a while, and try on another viewpoint instead.

Although the teen is still in the moral stage of Ideal Reciprocity (the Golden Rule), he is able to look beyond the face value of an action to evaluate it by the intentions, motives, social conditions, or life influences of the people responsible for the action. His definition of what's right may also shift. "Right" may become "what's right for the group."

But there's a caveat to reciprocity: researcher John C. Gibbs points out that "reciprocity can serve many masters – including hate."

Since one of the teen's strongest desires is to be accepted, his morality tends to be conformist. When he has a moral decision to make, he tends to ask, "What will *they* think of me if I do this (or if I don't do this)?" The *they* in question are the people who are significant to him. *They* might be his school peer group, a best friend, a teacher, a coach, parents, or other relatives. In any case, the significant people in his life are part of his moral compass.

Some young adults of high school and college age grow into an even more mature stage of morality in which they measure moral decisions by social norms or even in universal terms. These teens tend to be the more contemplative and principled in their age group. Their morality is part of their self-perception. It has become part of their identity.

SPIRITUALLY

Because the adolescent is trying to establish identity, the teen years are a time to personalize faith. Fowler says that in order to make faith personal and real, a teen needs to understand how the faith and/or spiritual views upheld by his faith community relate to all the areas of life he's involved in: family, school, peers, work, the media, church groups, hobbies, and other interests. Faith, even the belief in atheism, "must provide a basis for identity and outlook" and must be able to function not only in the area of the unseen but also in the realm of practical interactions with the world.

During this stage, questions and tension abound. The teen does not want to simply imitate his parents' or friends' faith anymore but wants to develop strong beliefs of his own. He wants to have his own beliefs, his own values, and his own faith. Teens, then, may rebel against their previous taken-for-granted beliefs, not necessarily in the sense of revolting but in the sense of refusing to "buy in." This opens the way to finding a personal spiritual belief.

WHEN YOU WRITE

All coming of age novels show the struggle for identity in a time-limited frame. Kelly Bingham, a YA writer and mother of teens, speaking at the Southern Festival of Books, shared a list of some of these struggles. She says that a teen protagonist often enters his story with one or more of the following:

self-doubt

bitterness

anger

self-centeredness

jealousy

depression

guilt

refusing to mature

blaming others for their problems

wondering where they fit in

wondering "who am I?"

The adversity that the teen faces in the novel at first creates a surge of self-doubt and no obvious way forward, says Kelly. By the end of the story, the teen has worked through his problems, although he usually has more maturing to do. But at least he has learned one or more positive traits, possibly resourcefulness or courage, maybe empathy for others or the ability to ask for help. Perhaps he learned gratitude, resilience, hope, a conscious choice to mature, self-awareness, or was inspired to make a conscious search for who he is and where he belongs. Whatever the teen protagonist has learned, it's a positive trait that brings him hope. It's something he can cling to in the future when life gets tough.

But how do these changes come about in a protagonist? Through hardship, pain, and problems. "Only when the loneliness becomes unbearable do adolescents root themselves, or try to root themselves," says Orson Scott Card. "It may or may not be in the community of their childhood, and it may or may not be their childhood identity and connections that they resume upon entering adulthood."

If you write YA, or if young adults play an important role in your novel, then read some current YA novels that are known for portraying teen struggles and teen voices.

Thirteen to Twenty

- questioning and tension
- personalizing faith/spirituality
- adult reasoning
- alert to the expectations of others
- conformist morality

Conflict: Identity vs. Identity Confusion

Strength: Fidelity

9.
The Twenties

CONFLICT: INTIMACY VS. ISOLATION

STRENGTH: LOVE

The Transition into Adulthood

New Adult books (NA), featuring eighteen- to twenty-five-year-old protagonists, mark the transition from YA books to the adult category. So to help us cross the bridge into the adult stages, we'll look at what characterizes "new adults."

Deborah Halverson of DearEditor.com wrote of this age group, "They're finally ditching the baggage of family and childhood associations, but they're doing so before the risk-taking and decision-making part of their brain is fully wired. That's not complete until age twenty-five. Until then, new adults remain as susceptible to peer pressure as teens – only now they lack adult censorship." She points out that new adults' "worldviews expand as they get to live that independent life they craved," but "grandiose expectations from teenhood clash with harsh reality." So the transition from adolescence into adulthood is marked by making commitments regarding typical adult life choices, such as career, serious romantic relationships, and personal lifestyle.

Since we, as writers, are interested in creating realistic hardships and struggles for our characters, let's consider the baggage an adolescent might carry into adulthood.

Role confusion: If a new adult leaves adolescence with *identity confusion*, uncertain of her beliefs, values, goals, and dreams, she will continue to search for her identity in adulthood. That makes it difficult for her to make the commitments that characterize this new stage. Even when she does make a commitment, for example to a relationship, her focus remains on herself, which makes for a lopsided relationship that she will have a hard time maintaining. Erikson called this *role confusion*.

Role diffusion: According to Erikson, this simply means she makes no commitments.

Role foreclosure: Her identity is swallowed up in someone else's identity. Perhaps her major life choices were made for her by parents or coaches or religion or government (as in a military draft). On one hand, she may feel relieved, because she doesn't have to risk making a wrong choice, so she may gladly relinquish the responsibility for those decisions to others. On the other hand, she may feel frustrated and, on some level, wish she could choose her own path, but she succumbs to the pressure to accept someone else's choice.

Moratorium: She may postpone making life choices, perhaps by getting more education, or traveling to "find herself," or serving in the Peace Corp or some other mission focused group. Of course, not everyone who continues their education or travels or serves in a mission group does it for the purpose of postponing life choices. But for a person still unsure of his identity, those can be ways to avoid other commitments.

Add to these the positives and negatives, strengths and weaknesses a character developed in the previous stages, and we have a complex, believable adult. Of course, being an adult comes with its own challenges, as we'll see in all three of the adult stages.

Emotionally

Intimacy develops when we have a friend in whom we can confide, someone who sticks with us in spite of our weaknesses and flaws. Because an intimate relationship is reciprocal, we know the other person's weaknesses and flaws as well, but we commit to each other anyway. This applies not only to committed romantic relationships but also to close friendships of any type, including some group and work relationships.

Do online friends count? If you're writing contemporary stories, you'll want to consider the impact of social media. Sharing anything we want with "friends" 24/7 may give us the impression of intimacy, but is it? Peggy Orenstein, in her book *Cinderella Ate My Daughter*, quotes Adriana Manago, a researcher at the Children's Digital Media Center in L.A.: "The self becomes a brand, something to be marketed to others rather than developed from within. Instead of intimates with whom you interact for the sake of the exchange, friends become your consumers, an audience for whom you perform." Orenstein says, "Electronic media have created a series of funhouse mirrors. They both forge greater intimacy and undermine it – sometimes simultaneously." She points out that with social media, we risk "alienation from living, breathing friends, from the messiness and reciprocity of authentic relationships."

True intimacy comes from face to face relationships, which make us vulnerable in a different way. Partners in an intimate relationship know each other's character, not just image, and can hurt one another deeply. Taking that risk and allowing yourself to become that vulnerable requires a solid identity, a strong sense of self, which was the goal of adolescence. So the question is, did your character develop a strong sense of self in the teen years when, as Orenstein says, social media encouraged "self- promotion over self-awareness."

Intimacy requires compromise, risk of ego, and sometimes self-sacrifice. According to Erikson, a person who can't take that risk may try to destroy whatever threatens his boundaries. Even though he may be quite social, if he can't enter or maintain an intimate relationship, he is left with a sense of isolation. It's only when he accepts intimacy that he finds the strength of *love*, meaning the unconditional respect, support, care, and encouragement essential for keeping relational commitments.

MORALLY

Adults can get stuck in any of the previous stages. You may know adults who never stopped being egocentric. Others seem to have camped out in the basic reciprocity "eye for an eye" stage. Still others mature and now enter the stage of "mutuality," which reflects the challenge to establish intimate relationships of mutual trust and personal sharing.

From this point on, according to researcher Gibbs, people fall into one of two camps. They are either conventional Type A's or universalized Type B's. Type A conventionals think within the bounds of their social network, which means they make moral judgments based on existing social norms. Being good or nice is measured by those norms. As Gibbs puts it, people with "Type A judgment . . . can turn into moral marshmallows, willing to do something because 'everybody's doing it.'"

Type B universals think globally. Universalized caring is their ideal, and their judgments focus on "the way the world should be." They perceive themselves as moral individuals. Morality is a crucial part of their identity. "B's are more . . .

internal," says Gibbs, "centering their judgments" on their personal moral identity.

SPIRITUALLY

At this stage, faith/spirituality may stagnate and take a back seat to the consuming daily cares of life. Religious rites and rituals may simply become part of a lifestyle. On the other hand, spiritual beliefs may continue to grow. If that's the case, faith tends to cycle between periods of reflection and periods of recommitment. In other words, we ponder and evaluate our beliefs, perhaps doubting and questioning as we seek a greater understanding of the unseen or a deeper connection with the divine. Periodically we reach points at which we either recommit more deeply to what we previously believed, or we embrace a different spiritual path that rings true to where we find ourselves in life.

10.

Thirties through Sixties

CONFLICT: GENERATIVITY VS. STAGNATION

STRENGTH: CARE

<u>Emotionally</u>

IF WE REACH THIS POINT in our lives with a strong sense of identity and meaningful, intimate relationships, we can be responsible not only for ourselves but for other people as well. That's what generativity is all about. *Generativity* has a double meaning. In one sense it means we are highly productive at this time of life, generating goods, services, and ideas for society and taking our place in the ever-changing world. But generativity also implies a focus on *generations*. One major reason we're productive and generative is to provide for the next generation.

Our commitments now become more involved and complicated: parenting, teaching, establishing careers, making and enforcing laws, caring for the environment. We commit ourselves and our efforts to the good of generations to come and to a world we will not see. Making decisions for the good of others requires an outward focus. Erikson says that when we achieve generativity, we develop the strength of *care*.

The opposite of an outward focus is, of course, an inward focus: making decisions only for the good of self. A person who is unable to *generate* may be stuck wrestling with negative baggage she carried into this stage from earlier in life. In any case, if she is not generative, she *stagnates*.

Morally and Spiritually

Morality now usually centers on the common good. Mature middle-age adults accept and perpetuate certain standards, systems, and institutions for society. Type A's depend on authorities, laws, and social norms to guide their moral decisions. Type B's lean toward ideal moral law and focus on their individual contributions to creating a better society.

Faith and spirituality at this stage continue to cycle between reflecting and recommitting. However, at this point, faith is more mature and less idealistic. It includes accepting hardships as an ongoing reality of life.

11.

Older Adulthood

CONFLICT: INTEGRITY VS. DESPAIR

STRENGTH: WISDOM

EMOTIONALLY

SOME PEOPLE CONTINUE to be generative throughout older adulthood. But for most people, older adulthood brings a realization that major life choices have already been made, for better or worse, and that options from here on are more limited. Older adults realize that life was not a dress rehearsal but the onstage production, and each year that passes brings them closer to the curtain call.

Adjusting to these changes is the conflict during this last stage. I often say that each life is a story with a beginning, a middle, an end, and an echo. The echo is who we are, remembered. Older adulthood, then, is the time when we put the finishing touches on our identity. In *Listening to Your Life*, Frederick Buechner describes older adulthood this way: "[Y]ou don't have to prove yourself any longer. You can be who you are and say what you feel, and let the chips fall where they may."

According to Erikson, during this stage a person develops either an uplifting sense of *integrity* or a sinking sense of *despair*, depending on how he looks back on his life. Susan Cain, in her book *Quiet*, says that psychologist Dan McAdams believes, "Unhappy people tend to see setbacks as contaminants that ruined an otherwise good thing . . . while generative adults see them as blessings in disguise." Integrity is the "blessings in disguise" viewpoint. We *integrate* our identity from all the previous stages, recognizing our past choices, both right and wrong, as stepping stones to who we have become, and we're satisfied with the fullness of life, its ups and downs, its good times and bad. Integrity implies wholeness and truth, and at its deepest and richest, includes having no fear of death.

When older adults have a strong sense of integrity, younger generations (which includes middle age) tend to see them as *wise*. So the emotionally integrated older adult may have "followers" and accepts the responsibility that comes with influence. Erikson says, "Healthy children will not fear life if their elders have integrity enough not to fear death."

Of course, not every older adult experiences this final stage with a sense of integrity. On the negative side of the conflict is despair, which comes from looking back on life choices with regret. Despair shows up in older adults as bitterness and depression. They may complain and blame others for what went wrong in their lives. They may fear death and become grasping and greedy at the end.

<u>Morally and Spiritually</u>

At this stage, faith/spirituality can include the deeper understandings that grow out of a variety of life experiences. Older adults who are still maturing morally (as opposed to settling into a previous stage) may move beyond an interest in the "common good." If researchers are right, not many people advance higher than that. If they do, the next stage is principle focused, which includes an interest in moral theory, universal or natural rights, and what's best for the greatest number of people.

But it's possible to move higher morally. The next rung up the moral ladder is for those who tend toward the philosophical and make deep, thoughtful, reasoned moral judgments. The highest moral stage is achieved by only a few. Labeled "cosmic," this stage is reached only through deep thought and soul searching, although it may be brought on by a crisis, such as a near death experience. People at the cosmic level commit their lives to humanitarian action inspired by love and respect for humanity. (Think Mother Teresa or Gandhi or the Dalai Lama.) They stand for and live as examples of the highest ideals: love, peace, kindness, goodness, grace, and mercy. These are their keys to deeper reality. Theirs is a wisdom the world recognizes, seeks, and honors.

Practical and Cultural Considerations

THE PRACTICAL

YOU DON'T NEED TO BE an expert on any of these stages or memorize them or turn them into rules. Sometimes the most interesting stories are about characters who *don't* fit the norm – kids who are precocious or adults who act morally like preschoolers. Being aware of the stages simply helps us make informed choices about our characters. We can write with intention and create believable characters who make moral choices and struggle with age-appropriate emotional crises.

Character-driven novels are based on the reality that we don't have to carry emotional baggage all our lives. That's one of the fascinating aspects of this type of novel: showing us that life has a way of giving us many chances to deal with our issues. So consider ways in which the negative at each stage can add to the baggage your character carries into subsequent stages. That baggage is part of your character's backstory, affecting each succeeding stage until you force her to confront and deal with her issues. As readers, when we see characters deal with their issues, we often find the courage to deal with our own.

CULTURAL CONSIDERATIONS

So do these stages hold true across cultures? The answer is yes, but . . .

EMOTIONALLY

Erikson believed that his stages crossed cultural barriers but were shaded, as we would logically expect, by the worldview of each culture. His stages show how each of us becomes who we are, how we gain our identity. But E. Mavis Hetherington and Ross D. Parke in *Child Psychology*, point out that identity is viewed differently in different cultures. In Western European and North American cultures, "identity is largely determined by personal accomplishments. In contrast, in collective societies, like China, Japan, and Native American tribes, a greater proportion of a person's identity is related to his or her membership in the larger group."

That difference in orientation – toward the individual or the community – seems to be one of the major variations between cultures. In some cultures parents value and teach cooperation, interdependence, and loyalty to the extended family. In others, parents train children toward self-reliance, competition, and achievement.

Mentally

The individual/community difference also shows up in how various cultures value cognitive skills. According to Hetherington and Parke, researcher Pierre Dasin found that "people value and develop 'those skills and concepts that are useful in the daily activities required' by their ecocultural settings." In some cultures honesty, respect, and serving the community are of greater value than cognitive skills, which are valued only if they're used to serve the group.

Even thought processes can vary from culture to culture. For example, some cultures think wholistically while others think analytically. Wholistic thinking is the process of understanding parts by first seeing the pattern of the whole. Analytic thinking is understanding the whole by first looking at the parts. What does this have to do with us as writers? It's a good example of the conflict we can create by placing a person from one culture into a culture that is foreign to him. Hetherington and Parke point out that there are "difficulties for children raised in one culture when they must attend school and prepare to work and function socially in a culture in which a different cognitive style is dominant."

Morally

What about morality? According to researcher John Gibbs, most societies reach at least stage three of moral development, which is the "mutuality" of late adolescence and early adulthood. (That's when people become either the "social norms" Type A or the universal, "the way the world should be" Type B.) For a culture to climb higher on the moral ladder, certain conditions have to exist. 1) The culture's social norms have to reflect and support the higher values. 2) Its institutions have to be interdependent, working toward common goals. 3) Morality has to become internalized ("this is who we are – a society of high moral values").

Most cultures also have some religious tradition or philosophy that professes basic reciprocity, or what we sometimes call the Golden Rule: "Do unto others as you would have them do unto you" (Christianity, Bible, Matthew 7:1). In Hinduism it's, "This is the sum of duty: do naught unto others that you would not have them do unto you" (Mahabharata 5, 1517). In Buddhism, "Hurt not others in ways that you yourself would find hurtful" (Udana-Varga 5,1). In Judaism, "That which is hateful to you, do not do to your fellow. That is the whole Torah; the rest is explanation" (Rabbi Hillel, Talmud)

Spiritually

Religion is the foundation of some cultures. In those societies, rites, rituals, and holy days are an integral part of the lifestyle. For many people in such cultures, whether or not they fully believe the teachings of that religion, they take part in its cultural expressions. It's a crucial part of their identity and their link to their community.

When You Write

Be aware. Gender roles can be culture specific. So can parenting styles. But when you get culture-specific, make sure your characters are fully rounded individuals, and avoid stereotyping. The bottom line is, if you're unsure about a particular culture, do your homework so that your characters accurately reflect their culture.

Part Two

The Enneagram for Writers

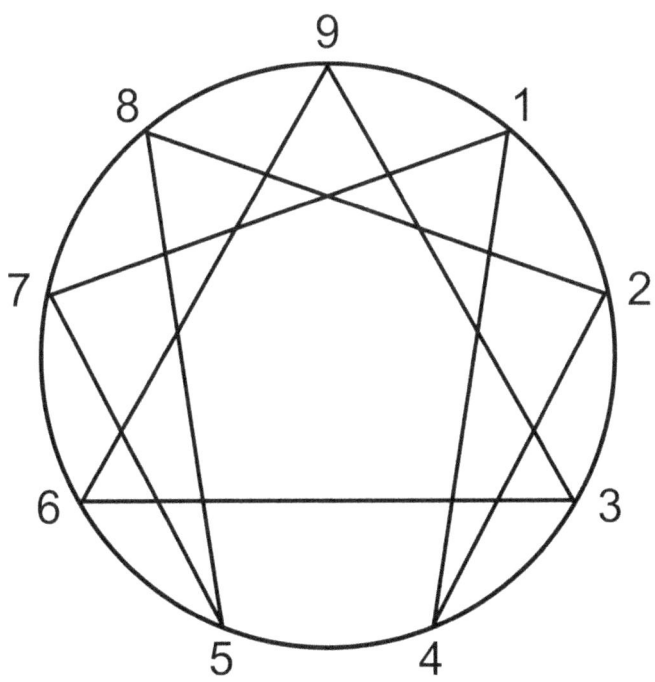

13.

Overview and Tips to Keep in Mind

LET'S BEGIN with a brief walk-through of what you'll find in this section and how it applies to your writing.

Each of nine personality types is described under the following headings.

I VALUE IN MYSELF AND OTHERS:

These are the values that the character considers essential to his well-being and by which he measures himself and others.

PERSONAL GOAL AND DESIRE:

In a character-driven novel, the protagonist will struggle toward both an external goal and an internal goal. The personal, internal struggle is our focus in this section. The protagonist may or may not reach her personal goal by the end of the story. She may, in fact, discover that her original goal has actually been hindering her. If so, she may modify this goal or trade it for a goal that fits her better as she changes throughout the course of the story.

It may help to think of this personal goal and desire as a need or yearning. David Corbett says in *The Art of Character*, "We long for something else, something better, something deeper and purer and truer, even if we have no clear idea what that might be, or how to go about naming it, let alone finding it. And as writers we transmit that yearning to our characters." It's this longing that drives a character. This is her personal goal and desire.

My controlling belief:

Controlling beliefs can be true or false. Even false beliefs have power, because we act not according to what is true but according to what we perceive is true. "It is the mind that maketh good or ill, that maketh wretch or happy, rich or poor," wrote Edmund Spenser. So, true or false, your character's controlling beliefs guide him as he makes decisions.

Characters don't easily let go of core beliefs. But that makes for a good story. Plots often begin with the protagonist holding false controlling beliefs. Events then challenge those beliefs, leading the character to realize that they're false.

My fear:

The character's fear is linked to her value, her inner goal and desire, and her controlling belief. For example, if she believes that she must be perfect in order to win her father's acceptance and love, she will fear appearing imperfect. Whatever she fears will hold her back and become a barrier to getting what she really wants or needs. This applies to antagonists as well as protagonists. It's especially insightful to discover what your antagonist's fear is.

Subtypes:

You can differentiate two characters of the same general type by making them different subtypes. This will set up tension and conflict between the two, even if they are allies.

>Group-oriented: This person enjoys large groups and has lots of friends.

>Intimacy-oriented: This person prefers small groups and a few close friends.

>Self-oriented: This person prefers solitude.

My mask:

"Everyone is a moon, and has a dark side which he never shows to anybody," wrote Mark Twain. If everyone is a moon, then the bright side is the image our characters show the world. But if that's all readers see, we have flat characters. Add the dark side, for well-rounded character.

The words *dark side* may conjure a picture of evil, but most of the time our dark side is simply the fears and weaknesses we don't want anyone else to see. Sometimes we hide our dark side so well it becomes a blind spot. Even we don't see it.

To describe the hidden dark side, many writers use the metaphor of a mask. At the beginning of a story, the protagonist is "masked," protecting himself from what he most fears: rejection – the loss of love and/or respect (including position, power, or influence). If he's a nurturer, he may fear that if he cannot be of help, he won't be worthy of love and respect. So his mask is caregiving, serving so thoroughly that he becomes indispensible. He never admits his own needs.

"True character waits behind this mask," says Robert McKee in *Story*. It's our job as writers to challenge our protagonists to remove the mask and become people with personal integrity.

Good Angel/Bad Angel and Neutral:

In any given situation, your character can choose to respond at her worst, at her best, or in neutral.

Remember the cartoons in which a character has an angel sitting on one shoulder and a devil on the other? In real life, our most wrenching decisions are often made after wrestling with issues that lie in a gray area, not angel or devil, right or wrong, but uncertain. We identify with characters who struggle over choosing the better of two good options, or the lesser of two evils.

We also identify with characters who wrestle with their beliefs in situations that pit their good angel vs. their bad angel. These inner conflicts of conscience not only make a character believable but also make us care. Of course, no person is perfectly good or perfectly evil. We all can choose at any one moment to listen to the positive or the negative. So even if your character is unlikeable, give him or her at least one positive trait. That includes antagonists. The converse applies as well: Even a good character will have one or more flaws.

Good angel and bad angel are often two sides of the same coin, the coin being the character's type. For example, with Type 1, the perfectionist, her good angel holds high ideals and desires justice. But flip the coin, and her bad angel shows up, judgmental and hypocritical. Her strength is her weakness. Two sides of the perfectionist coin.

1. AT MY WORST, I am . . .

    <u>My Weakness is</u> . . .

For protagonists: The "worst" or "weakness" can function as your character's flaw, the emotionally immature area from which she will be challenged to grow as your story progresses. This weakness, along with her fear, is what she will mask.

For antagonists: The "worst" can be the foundation from which an antagonist functions, the place where he is stuck and refuses to change.

For allies and enemies: The "worst" can be the mode of any character, ally, or enemy who creates obstacles that thwart your maturing protagonist and tempt her to return to her previous, more immature behavior. Or these characters, by their own immature or inappropriate behavior, can place your protagonist in danger.

2. In neutral, I am . . .

This is the default position, one your protagonist takes when she's in normal mode and not under pressure.

3. At my best, I am . . .

    <u>My Strengths are</u> . . .

Characters who operate at their best tend to be the mentors of the story, the wise friends or counselors. They may even be former heroes from your backstory, people your protagonist admires or hopes to emulate as he or she becomes heroic. Which brings us to:

BACKSTORY:

This section suggests general events that may have contributed to your character's personality type. While some traits seem to be inborn, natural temperaments (like a sunny or stormy disposition, introversion or extroversion), many other factors are involved in personality as well: the environment he grew up in, the beliefs he was taught, his education, and his life experiences. It's important to know each main character's backstory, because that affects his or her point of view in every scene. When you write, you will include only the character background that will move the story forward. Even then you will place backstory only where the reader needs to know it. As a result, you'll never tell your reader everything you know about your characters. But even what you don't reveal will fuel your writing, and you may discover that a bit of backstory you thought you wouldn't use actually makes a nice twist later in your plot.

Stubborn stance:

Early in your story, at the first sign of pressure, your main character usually responds with his or her stubborn stance, which does not help matters at all. In fact, his stubborn stance often backfires, bringing on more pressure. But as the story unfolds, his mask lowers, and he abandons the immature, stubborn stance that no longer works. Your protagonist matures. Which brings us to the last description of type, which is tremendously helpful for a character-driven story.

To leave my weakness and grow into my strength, I must learn to:

This is the character's emotional arc. Author James Scott Bell says, "Our great task in life is to do battle with our frailties and overcome them." So this section suggests emotional stepping-stones that this particular type of character must cross in order to reach a place of strength and stability by the end of your story.

After the description of each personality type, I list a couple of characters from the Angelaeon Circle series, in case you want to see how the type plays out in a novel.

One warning: Any kind of character study, including the Enneagram, can paralyze you. If you're not careful you can find yourself referring to this model as a list that, instead of freeing your character to create the story, chains the character to requirements. The truth is, weaving plot threads together into a story requires a loose hand. As your novel progresses, you may discover that your character is not the type you thought she was. You may need to return to the Enneagram to find out who she really is.

To avoid this problem, you may want to do what I did and write a rough draft *before* turning to the Enneagram. With a complete rough draft, I knew the basics about my characters. Then I fleshed them out more deeply with the Enneagram.

On the other hand, there are advantages to using the Enneagram to create your characters from scratch before writing a single word. The major advantage is that the personalities and motivations inspired by your character's type can help you create the plot. We'll cover those specifics in Part Three.

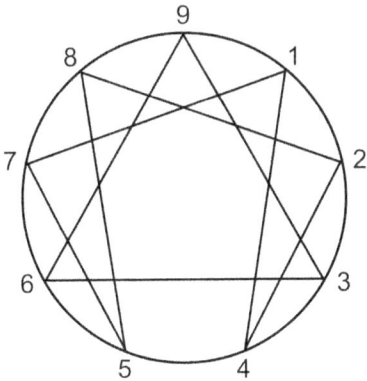

14.

Type 1
Perfectionist - Reformer - Renovator

I VALUE IN MYSELF AND OTHERS: hard work, integrity, being organized

MY PERSONAL GOAL AND DESIRE: perfection

MY CONTROLLING BELIEF is that being perfect will bring me security. The closer to perfect I am, the more I am worthy of love and respect.

MY FEAR: being seen as less than perfect (I avoid this at all costs.)

SUBTYPES (choose one):

GROUP-ORIENTED:

I enjoy sharing my group's beliefs.

I want to work with others to reform the system.

INTIMACY-ORIENTED:

I have high standards for relationships.

I can be jealous, afraid of losing my friend(s) to someone more perfect.

I can be controlling.

SELF-ORIENTED:

I worry about my safety.

I am afraid of errors, mistakes, and failure.

I can be hesitant when I speak, self-correcting as I go.

MY MASK: strict control of my reactions, hiding anger and resentment

Good Angel/Bad Angel and Neutral:

1. <u>At my worst</u>, I am angry and resentful toward people who don't live up to my standards. I may be:

    over-sensitive to criticism

    disappointed in myself

    judgmental toward myself and others

    over-sensitive to the imperfections in others and in social systems

    a moralistic know-it-all; a fault-finder; self-righteous

    a workaholic

    serious and slow to relax and enjoy life

    hypocritical (I may talk/act morally in public but live immorally in private.)

    denying myself "lesser" pleasures to make sure I take the moral high ground

    repressing my own needs; even my hobbies are done for the benefit of others

    unable to forgive my own guilt over past failures

    unable to accept unconditional love

MY WEAKNESS: anger

> When my goals are frustrated, I get annoyed. When pushed, I get angry.

2. IN NEUTRAL, I am serious, perfectionistic, idealistic, and meticulous.

3. AT MY BEST, I am cheerful, patient, and fair. I can be:

   a principled person with high standards

   just and fair, considering all sides of an issue or cause

   diligent in working to make the world a better place

   organized

   honest

   self-controlled

   inspirational and motivational, able to teach others

   balanced

   MY STRENGTH: having high ideals

   > I truly yearn for a just and moral world.

BACKSTORY

(These are general suggestions. You'll want to come up with your own specifics.)

As a child, she tried to please, to behave, to be good in order to earn love. Or to avoid punishment. She became an achiever, trying to live up to high expectations.

She may have had a strong religious education.

She earnestly absorbed what was taught as good and bad, right and wrong, and used that as a measuring stick for herself and others. Those voices became loud in her mind.

Caregiver(s) may have responded with conditional love. Perhaps they were perfectionists themselves, quick to lecture or moralize, slow to praise, and never satisfied with her best efforts.

If caregiver(s) were absent or irresponsible, she had to take on caregiving responsibility for her family. She felt pressure to be a protector, provider, and role model for younger siblings.

MY STUBBORN STANCE: I am right.

To leave my weakness and grow into my strength, I must learn to:

rest, relax, chill out

accept the fact that everyone is imperfect, including me

enjoy the process more than the end goal

grant grace and mercy to myself and others

laugh at myself

give up wanting all or nothing

direct my anger toward restoring justice

play, recreate, and enjoy life

recognize and accept unconditional love

Angelaeon Circle type 1 characters:

Hanamel (Hanni), introduced in *Breath of Angel*

King Kedemeth, introduced in *Eye of the Sword*

Writing Deep, Believable Characters | 107

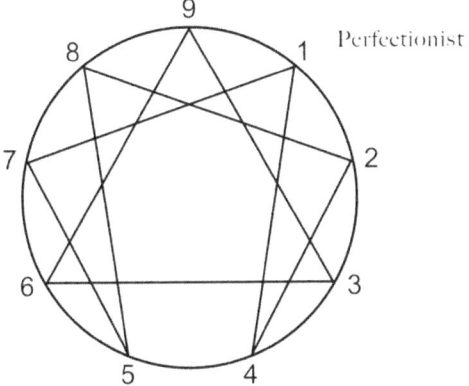

Type 2
Nurturer – Helper – Caregiver

I VALUE IN MYSELF AND OTHERS: helpfulness

MY PERSONAL GOAL AND DESIRE: to be noticed and valued for helping

MY CONTROLLING BELIEF is that taking care of people, "fixing" their situations, will bring me security. The more helpful and selfless I am, the more I am worthy of love and respect.

MY FEAR: being rejected; not being needed (I avoid this at all costs.)

SUBTYPES (choose one):

GROUP-ORIENTED:

I am ambitious and want to be influential.

I want to be valuable to the group.

I want to be close to and help "important people."

INTIMACY-ORIENTED:

I do whatever I can to be wanted and needed in a relationship.

I work hard to overcome obstacles in relationships.

SELF-ORIENTED:

I want to be acknowledged, thanked, and rewarded for my helpfulness.

I want to be in the forefront helping so I can feel good about myself.

MY MASK: self-sufficiency, appearing to be in control; hiding the fact that I am needy (Helping others can be a way to avoid dealing with my own needs.)

Good Angel/Bad Angel and Neutral:

1. <u>At my worst</u>, I am either overbearing and presumptuous or clingy and possessive. I may:

   jump into situations in which I can help without being asked

   feel taken for granted or feel like a martyr if my efforts aren't appreciated

   resent how much I do for others and feel superior to those I help

   refuse to admit my own needs and neglect or avoid self-care

   flatter others to manipulate them into letting me help them

   take pride in being indispensable

   control others by taking care of them

   find it impossible to say no

   promise more than I can deliver

   link my identity to the people I help and to how they react

   change, chameleon-like, to fit the needs of others

   blame others when I fall short

> My Weakness: pride, expecting others to be grateful for all I do for them
>
> When I'm hurt, I can be vicious.

2. In neutral, I'm sensitive and emotional. I actively care for, give to, and "mother" people, hoping to be noticed. I like to snuggle, discuss relationships, and talk about love.

3. At my best, I am humble, friendly, and caring. I can:

> share, give, and help generously
>
> compliment and encourage others
>
> feel good when I help others succeed
>
> adapt easily
>
> be a faithful friend
>
> love, not expecting or demanding anything in return
>
> sense when my tendency to help will not be helpful
>
> My Strength: compassion and care

Backstory

(These are general suggestions. You'll want to come up with your own specifics.)

As he grew up, helping may have been a condition for being noticed and loved.

He may not have felt as secure as he needed to feel.

He may have felt that he had to emotionally support one or more members of the family, including the adult(s).

He may have felt that his caregiver was weak, which made him the responsible, strong one in the relationship.

My stubborn stance: I am the only one who is able to help.

To leave my weakness and grow into my strength, I must learn to:

    stop manipulating people and situations

    make sure the people I help actually want my help

    let go of people once I have helped them

    help others anonymously

practice stepping back and letting someone else help

let my head rule my heart

figure out who I am as an individual apart from those who need help

stop clinging to others and stand on my own

admit and express my own brokenness and needs

let others help me

Angelaeon Circle type 2 characters:

Queen Ambria, introduced in *Eye of the Sword*

Serai, introduced in *Breath of Angel*

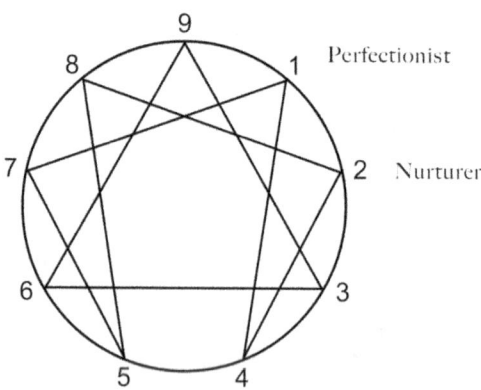

16.

Type 3
Producer – Achiever – Ace

I VALUE IN MYSELF AND OTHERS: achievement and success

MY PERSONAL GOAL AND DESIRE: to be successful

MY CONTROLLING BELIEF is that success will bring me security. The more successful I am, the more I am worthy of love and respect.

MY FEAR: failure (I avoid this at all costs.)

SUBTYPES (choose one):

   GROUP-ORIENTED:

      I want to be in the right groups and meet their standards.

I can usually get people to work well together, successfully networking them.

Intimacy-oriented:

I value romantic relationships.

My self-image depends on how successfully I play my role in a relationship.

Self-oriented:

I feel most secure when I succeed at my skills or position.

I work hard to achieve and to avoid failure.

I crave status for my self-esteem.

My mask: maintaining the appearance of success at all costs; putting a positive spin on what might otherwise be perceived as negative

Good Angel/Bad Angel and Neutral:

1. <u>At my worst</u>, I am dishonest and refuse to acknowledge failure. I may:

    be opportunistic

    be addicted to my career or role in life

    focus on image, be superficial, vain

    be completely "allergic" to failure

    deflect criticism

    give the impression that I'm succeeding even if I'm failing

    hide my true self behind roles, taking on whatever role portrays success

    visualize life as competitive; you either win or lose

    turn conversations toward my past successes

    turn hatred of failure into hatred of self if I can't escape a true failure

MY WEAKNESS: deception and blame

> When my goals are frustrated, I distance myself from failure by blaming someone/something besides me or reframing failure as a partial success.

2. IN NEUTRAL, I am competent and practical. I'm energized by success, which easily attracts people, and I enjoy being in front of groups, even crowds.

3. AT MY BEST, I am honest and accept failure as part of life. I can be:

> content without status and recognition
>
> capable and trustworthy
>
> confident and optimistic
>
> gregarious, mixing well with all types of people
>
> astute, able to discern when someone is being less than truthful
>
> busy and efficient
>
> willing to work hard to accomplish goals
>
> dynamic and productive

willing to step back and allow other people to get the credit for success

instrumental in helping other people succeed

<u>My Strength</u>: embracing failure as a stepping stone to success

Backstory

(These are general suggestions. You'll want to come up with your own specifics.)

Her caregiver(s) may have given praise, rewards, and love only when she was successful.

She learned to deflect blame in order to wiggle out of reprimands or punishment.

Achievements in competitive areas like sports, academics, or music may have given her an emotional high that she tries to duplicate as often as possible.

Her successes may have set a standard that she feels obligated to try to keep up.

She may have become "super kid" to try to live up to high expectations.

Her successes may have placed her in a group or clique that she once admired from afar, and now she believes failure would remove her from her hard-won position in the group.

Her success may have opened the door to the advancement of her family, and she feels the pressure to keep that door open by continuing to succeed.

Because she put took on the role of the achiever in order to appear successful, she may not really know herself. She may question who she really is.

MY STUBBORN STANCE: I achieve. I will not even entertain the possibility of failure.

TO LEAVE MY WEAKNESS AND GROW INTO MY STRENGTH, I MUST LEARN TO:

- stop craving the recognition of others

- be honest with myself and others

- accept criticism

- not abandon or run from failure

- take responsibility for my part, and only my part, in both success and failure practice solitude and not fear being alone

face failure and defeat as a normal part of life

discover and admit my true feelings

train myself to be a person of integrity

Angelaeon type 3 characters:

Lord Beker, introduced in *Breath of Angel*

Trevin, introduced in *Breath of Angel*

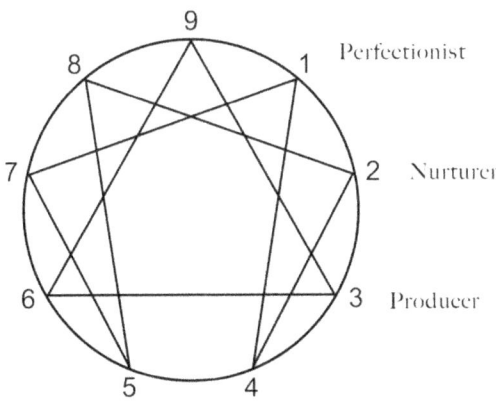

Type 4
Artist – Individualist – Romantic

I VALUE IN MYSELF AND OTHERS: uniqueness

MY PERSONAL GOAL AND DESIRE: to be unique

MY CONTROLLING BELIEF is that being unique will get me noticed and make me worthy of love and respect.

MY FEAR: conformity; fading into obscurity (I avoid this at all costs.)

SUBTYPES (choose one):

GROUP-ORIENTED:

I'm very conscious about or afraid of what others think of me.

I'm concerned that I won't measure up to the group's standards.

I act charming in order to avoid social pressure.

INTIMACY-ORIENTED:

I'm competitive in relationships.

I may be jealous, fearing that someone more attractive will replace me.

I long (and enjoy longing) for the perfect relationship.

SELF-ORIENTED:

I stubbornly insist on being unusual, unique, and special.

I may withdraw, feeling misunderstood and sorry for myself.

My mask: being special and unique at any cost; equating myself with my art

Good Angel/Bad Angel and Neutral:

1. <u>At my worst</u>, I am self-pitying, envious, and eccentric. I may:

    find satisfaction by feeling hurt, playing the misunderstood artist

    feel like an outsider

    compare myself to others who seem more normal, attractive, interesting, etc.

    be different simply for the sake of being different

    be angry at myself, self-critical

    be attracted to what's forbidden

    avoid what I see as ugly, dirty, or even ordinary

    feel that normal social standards don't apply to me

    <u>My Weakness</u>: envy

    > When my goals are frustrated, I feel sorry for myself and have a pity party.
    > When pushed, I get depressed.

2. <u>In neutral</u>, I curate and create beauty. I'm a moody, stylish romantic.

3. <u>At my best</u>, I am balanced, emotionally deep, and authentically creative. I am:

    able to understand the depths of the human soul, the emotions of others

    able to deal with the dark depths of others, because I've been there

    able to turn loss into beauty and universal meaning

    attracted to the energy of life

    artistically expressive

    able to easily detect what's authentic

    sensitive to symbolism, dreams, and the unseen

    <u>My Strength</u>: being authentically unique

Backstory

(These are general suggestions. You'll want to come up with your own specifics.)

He may have often experienced the present as being unbearable and meaningless.

He may have sustained a painful loss (physical or emotional) when he was young.

He may be hiding some kind of shame.

He may have experienced and deeply felt a range of emotions from heavy grief to high delight.

He may have lacked positive role models, so his identity turned inward.

He may have compensated for the love of weak or absent caregivers by cultivating a rich imagination.

My stubborn stance: I am an original and will always be different.

To leave my weakness and grow into my strength, I must learn to:

confront my loss, mourn it, grow from it, and move on

practice real love

appreciate the ordinary

balance my feelings and responses to be less extreme and dramatic

balance my imagination with reality

try to live in the present

be authentic, truly original

Angelaeon Circle type 4 characters:

Dio, introduced in *Eye of the Sword*

Prince Varic, introduced in *Eye of the Sword*

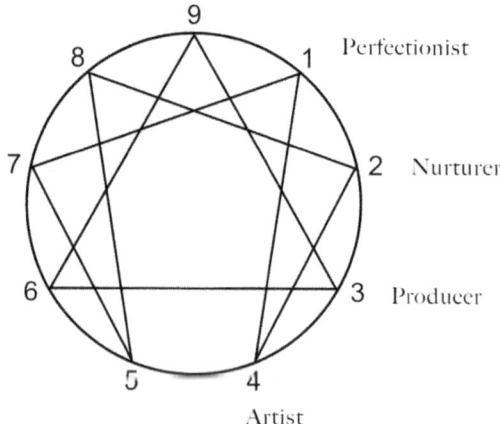

Type 5
Contemplative – Observer – Thinker

I VALUE IN MYSELF AND OTHERS: knowledge and wisdom

MY PERSONAL GOAL AND DESIRE: to know and understand

MY CONTROLLING BELIEF is that knowledge, understanding, and wisdom will bring me security, respect, and love.

MY FEAR: emptiness; misunderstanding and being misunderstood (I avoid this at all costs.)

SUBTYPES (choose one):

GROUP-ORIENTED:

I value "insider" knowledge and want to belong to a group of seekers.

I want to learn from and be valued by an expert.

INTIMACY-ORIENTED:

I tend to share with only one person.

I like to communicate with few words and have this person understand me.

SELF-ORIENTED:

I need private space, a refuge to withdraw to, so that I can recharge.

I'm perfectly content to observe and think alone for long periods of time.

MY MASK: withdrawal

Good Angel/Bad Angel and Neutral:

1. <u>At my worst</u>, I am isolated, obsessed with learning and collecting ideas. I may:

    be detached and withdrawn, avoiding attention

    try to fill the emptiness I feel with knowledge

    be reluctant to express feelings; I may seem emotionally cold

    see the company of others as an intrusion

    think I'm secure only when I'm fully informed

    keep my knowledge, wisdom, and even my emotions to myself

    be arrogant and conceited

    <u>My Weakness</u>: being a loner; hoarding knowledge and wisdom for myself

    When my goals are frustrated, I detach and withdraw.

2. <u>In neutral</u>, I am an observer and a brilliant thinker, maybe even a philosopher or mystic. I control my emotions.

3. <u>At my best</u>, I am perceptive, wise, and intellectually vibrant. I can:

> be objective
>
> focus my interest and attention on discovering and exploring what's new
>
> come up with profound and uncommon insights.
>
> be a good listener and observer
>
> counsel wisely and help others gain insight
>
> have a strong, quiet, inner strength
>
> <u>My Strength</u>: discovering and applying knowledge and wisdom

Backstory

(These are general suggestions. You'll want to come up with your own specifics.)

She may have gotten the message early on that she was not wanted.

She may have experienced little tenderness and a lack of intimacy from caregivers.

Or she may have experienced the opposite: Family or caregivers may have invaded her space, physically or psychologically.

She may have grown up in confined surroundings so that her inner world was the only space in which she could move freely, undisturbed.

Her capacity to express feelings physically was stifled and left underdeveloped.

Her main experience in life consisted in not getting what she actually needed.

MY STUBBORN STANCE: I know. I understand. I need my privacy.

TO LEAVE MY WEAKNESS AND GROW INTO MY STRENGTH, I MUST LEARN TO:

- gain wisdom and knowledge not only by thinking but also by real experience
- act as well as think
- accept the company of others
- be willing to commit to relationships

be generous with sharing knowledge, possessions, and wisdom

be a good counselor

express emotions

love

ANGELAEON TYPE 5 CHARACTERS:

Arelin, introduced in *Eye of the Sword*

Melaia, introduced in *Breath of Angel*

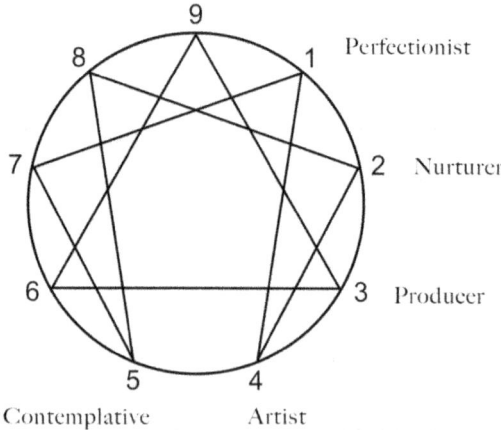

Type 6
Worrier – Skeptic – Doubter

I VALUE IN MYSELF AND OTHERS: loyalty

MY PERSONAL GOAL AND DESIRE: to do my duty and be loyal

MY CONTROLLING BELIEF is that upholding my duty and being loyal will bring me security, respect, and love.

MY FEAR: disorder and threats to stability (I avoid this at all costs.)

SUBTYPES (choose one):

GROUP-ORIENTED:

I am loyal and want the best for the group.

I am conservative and nervous about changes in the group.

INTIMACY-ORIENTED:

I want to appear strong and in control of relationships.

But I feel vulnerable and mistrusting.

SELF-ORIENTED:

I mistrust people, but I appear friendly to gain allies not enemies.

I may use humor to feel more secure.

MY MASK: strength and control

Good Angel/Bad Angel and Neutral:

1. <u>At my worst</u>, I am afraid and paranoid. I may:

    doubt myself and lack self-confidence

    follow an authority who can tell me where the limits are

    constantly sense danger and threat

    want to depend on others but mistrust them instead

    fear aggressors but be aggressive myself

    crave security but feel insecure

    set unreachable goals and actually find pleasure in failure

    be pessimistic, expecting the worst

    be suspicious of compliments or praise

    evade danger or invite danger

    <u>My Weakness</u>: anxiety and fear<u>:</u>

    > When my goals are frustrated, I am either cowardly and dependent or aggressive and reckless.

2. <u>IN NEUTRAL</u>, I am either authoritarian or anti-authoritarian. I'm interested in guidelines, rules, and law (I either protect it or break it). I like systems, structure, and order.

3. <u>AT MY BEST</u>, I am dependable and confident. I can:

   be a cooperative group member

   be warm, original, and humorous

   know what can and can't realistically be done

   be a visionary risk-taker

   sacrifice for those I love

   quickly, easily sense what's going on regarding both danger and opportunity

   stand up for the oppressed

   recognize and alleviate unfounded fears of others

   <u>MY STRENGTH</u>: courage

BACKSTORY

(These are general suggestions. You'll want to come up with your own specifics.)

He may have had caregivers who were uncontrolled, inconsistent, unpredictable, violent, or emotionally cold, which kept him from developing basic trust.

He may have been punished or beaten without a discernible cause.

He may have had to seek a caregiver he could trust.

He may have had to learn to anticipate or sense signs of danger and threat so he could protect himself.

He may have had to struggle with fear all his life.

He may not have been able to complete a course of training or study.

He may have reflected his caregivers' inconsistent behavior by becoming inconsistent himself, evoking the opposite of what he wanted: admiring authority but fearing it, fearing aggression but being aggressive, being likable sometimes but hateful at other times, embracing accepted values but undermining them, wanting to avoid punishment but earning it instead. In effect, he sabotages himself.

MY STUBBORN STANCE: I maintain order and control.

To leave my weakness and grow into my strength, I must learn to:

face my fear and talk about my feelings

acknowledge my exaggerated fears

allow myself to make mistakes

accept the fact that life issues are not all black and white but often gray

be comfortable with uncertainty and lack of order

trust myself and others

accept unconditional love

Angelaeon Circle type 6 characters:

Jarrod, introduced in *Breath of Angel*

Pym, introduced in *Breath of Angel*

Stalia, introduced in *Eye of the Sword*

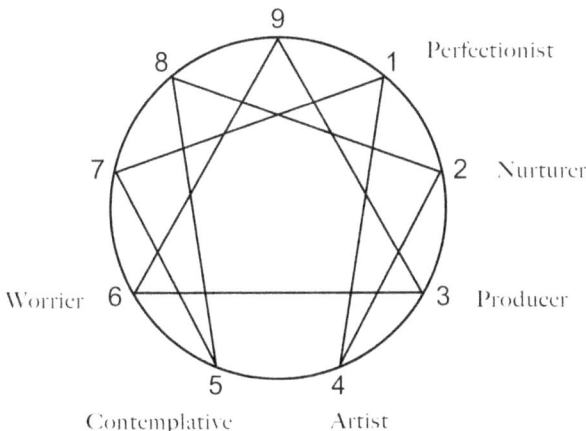

20.

Type 7
Adventurer – Bon Vivant – Zealot

I VALUE IN MYSELF AND OTHERS: pleasure and happiness

MY PERSONAL GOAL AND DESIRE: to find the joy in life

MY CONTROLLING BELIEF is that pleasure and happiness will fulfill me and bring me security, respect, and love.

MY FEAR: pain (I avoid this at all costs.)

SUBTYPES (choose one):

GROUP-ORIENTED:

> I am ready to sacrifice for the well-being and happiness of the group.

> I try to get everyone to see the positive and to be excited about the future.

INTIMACY-ORIENTED:

> I easily tire of relationships after the excitement and adventure wear off.

> I avoid difficulty and demands in relationships, preferring comfort and pleasure.

SELF-ORIENTED:

> I enthusiastically defend my goals.

> I choose to be around people who see life like I do and can have fun with me.

MY MASK: jokes, laughter, making light of problems, eternal optimism

GOOD ANGEL/BAD ANGEL AND NEUTRAL:

1. <u>AT MY WORST</u>, I am self-indulgent and excessive. I may:

    seek as much fun as possible

    stay busy with enjoyable tasks so I don't have to face my emptiness

    avoid or ignore pain, difficulty, and hard decisions

    deny or rationalize problems

    pretend to know it all

    be susceptible to addiction

    go over-the-top with whatever I think will lead to more happiness

    travel or change jobs often to keep life exciting and fun

    oppose realists who try to spoil my good mood, call them pessimists

    <u>MY WEAKNESS</u>: obsession with fleeting pleasures

    When my goals are frustrated, I repress that pain and seek more pleasure, perhaps with new, stimulating experiences.

2. <u>IN NEUTRAL</u>, I am cheerful, superficial, busy with useful but fun tasks.

3. <u>AT MY BEST</u>, I am clear-headed. I can:

> be optimistic, idealistic, and enthusiastic about the future
>
> adapt cheerfully
>
> be full of wonder at the gift of life
>
> see abundant beauty, goodness, and humor
>
> enjoy other people and help them enjoy life
>
> find joy without denying or avoiding life's hardships
>
> pursue and find a joy deeper than just pleasure
>
> help others find the joy in life

<u>MY STRENGTH</u>: deep joy

BACKSTORY

(These are general suggestions. You'll want to come up with your own specifics.)

She may have had traumatic experiences that she did not feel she could cope with.

Her caregivers may have shielded her, never allowing her to face problems, deal with difficult issues, or visit places that might challenge an all-is-well perspective of life.

She may have been spoiled with material gifts and pleasurable outings.

She may never have had to take on unpleasant tasks.

Or she may have been in dangerous or painful circumstances from which she escaped or was rescued, which led to her obsession with embracing pleasure in order to deny past pain and avoid future pain.

A controlling caregiver may have repeatedly told her that she couldn't handle problems and pain.

She may have been ignored and felt a deep emptiness that she found she could fill or escape, at least temporarily, with pleasure.

She may have had (or still have) weight problems.

MY STUBBORN STANCE: I am happy.

To leave my weakness and grow into my strength, I must learn to:

see and accept the whole of reality, pain as well as pleasure

be aware of my rationalizations

face my fear of pain, embrace and admit it

find deep joy by balancing optimism with an acceptance of hardship

Angelaeon Circle type 7 characters:

Dwin, introduced in *Breath of Angel*

Prince Resarian, introduced in *Eye of the Sword*

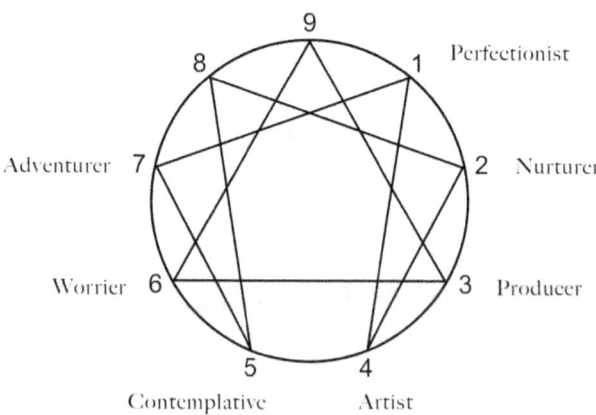

Type 8
Leader – Authority – Director

I VALUE IN MYSELF AND OTHERS: leadership

MY PERSONAL GOAL AND DESIRE: to take a stand and lead others

MY CONTROLLING BELIEF is that dominance and leadership will provide security and win me respect and love.

MY FEAR: being or appearing weak; isolation (I avoid this at all costs.)

SUBTYPES (choose one):

GROUP-ORIENTED:

I guide groups to bond in strong friendships.

I protect and support the weak in my community.

INTIMACY-ORIENTED:

I'm possessive about my partners and expect their wholehearted devotion.

I'm proud of my strength and toughness.

SELF-ORIENTED:

I try to control my environment.

I'm sensitive to the abuse of my rights.

MY MASK: strength

Good Angel/Bad Angel and Neutral:

1. <u>At my worst</u>, I am arrogant and power-hungry. I may:

    harshly judge myself and others

    see life as a hostile threat

    become confrontational, looking for – or stirring up – conflict

    become a tyrant, even a violent one

    never apologize

    mistrust others

    despise cowards (including my own vulnerability)

    become enraged if someone deceives or outmaneuvers me

    seek revenge to get justice

    <u>My Weakness</u>:

    When my goals are frustrated, I become aggressive and over-controlling.

2. **IN NEUTRAL,** I'm insecure and competitive. I want to stay informed and take charge so I can successfully guide my life and make sure that people who are important to me make the right decisions.

3. **AT MY BEST**, I am an assertive, protective, strong leader. I am:

   quick to sense dishonesty and injustice

   reliable, responsible, and trustworthy

   not afraid of conflict

   defensive and protective of the oppressed

   able to inspire others to follow me

   a lover of life

   committed to justice

   trustworthy

   MY STRENGTH: justice

Backstory

(These are general suggestions. You'll want to come up with your own specifics.)

In childhood, he may have experienced punishment for being weak and soft, so he hid his weakness and became strong and hard.

His caregivers may have taught him to fight back or strike first to show who's the boss.

He may have been bullied.

He may not have been able to trust anyone but himself.

He may have been challenged to prove his courage, facing formidable consequences if he failed.

He may have grown up under strict rules, and while he chafed under the control, he saw that the rule giver and enforcer demanded and received respect. So he decided to grow up to be the one giving orders and getting the respect.

MY STUBBORN STANCE: I am powerful and in control.

TO LEAVE MY WEAKNESS AND GROW INTO MY STRENGTH, I MUST LEARN TO:

realize how my aggression frightens and hurts others, alienating them

be merciful toward others

hold myself to the same standards that I expect from others

respect others as I want them to respect me

compromise

admit when I'm wrong and apologize

find nonviolent ways to use my position and power

ANGELAEON CIRCLE TYPE 8 CHARACTERS:

Benasin, introduced in *Breath of Angel*

Rejius, introduced in *Breath of Angel*

Writing Deep, Believable Characters | 155

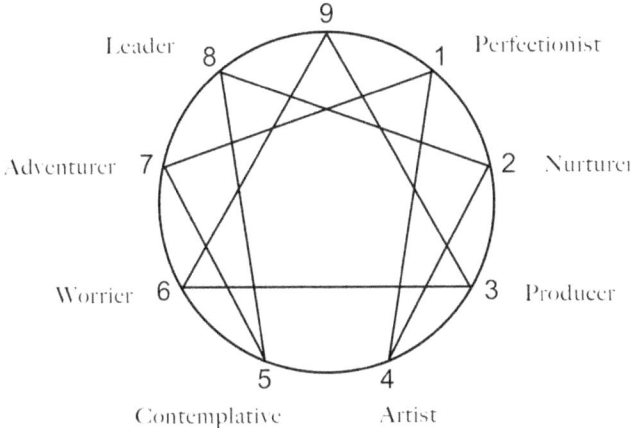

Type 9
Peacemaker – Diplomat – Mediator

I VALUE IN MYSELF AND OTHERS: calmness, balance

MY PERSONAL GOAL AND DESIRE: to live content with myself and in harmony with others

MY CONTROLLING BELIEF is that being at peace brings security, and being a peacemaker earns me respect and love.

MY FEAR: conflict (I avoid this at all costs.)

SUBTYPES (choose one):

GROUP-ORIENTED:

I want to belong.

I let others make the decisions, and I go along.

INTIMACY-ORIENTED:

I enjoy living through a partner.

I see my partner as ideal and refuse to see imperfections.

I enjoy being one with my partner

SELF-ORIENTED:

I overlook the difficulties and demands of the world.

I comfort or numb myself.

MY MASK: contentment

Good Angel/Bad Angel and Neutral:

1. <u>At my worst</u>, I am unfocused, overly humble, and stubborn. I may:

    procrastinate, especially when things are difficult or complicated

    fear my own greatness

    avoid confrontation, commitment, and decision-making

    withdraw and retreat, even from myself

    have a hard time completing projects

    want life to be simple, ruled by habits and routine

    take the path of least resistance

    <u>My Weakness</u>: laziness

    When my goals are frustrated, I resign myself to the situation and then numb and comfort myself, even to the point of addiction.

2. <u>In neutral</u>, I am adaptable. I go with the flow and avoid conflict. I may seem absent-minded.

3. **AT MY BEST**, I am easygoing, accepting, and peaceful. I can:

> function well as a mediator
>
> sense what is fair
>
> see issues from different points of view
>
> put others at ease
>
> avoid taking sides, without self-interest
>
> exude an inner peace
>
> speak truth calmly and persuasively

> MY STRENGTH: Action

BACKSTORY

(These are general suggestions. You'll want to come up with your own specifics.)

As a child, she may have felt overlooked or ignored. Her parents or siblings may have prioritized their interests over hers.

She may have been rejected if she expressed her opinion.

She may have been caught in the middle of two opposing sides (as in a marital dispute) and had to make her way between the two.

She may have been raised in a home in which conflict was avoided or swept under the rug.

She may have been spoiled and became comfortable with the status quo. Now she does not want to rock the boat.

My stubborn stance: I am content. Any problems will solve themselves in time.

To leave my weakness and grow into my strength, I must learn to:

    discern and respect my own feelings and desires

    discover and honor my viewpoints and gifts

    realize my self-worth

    complete projects on a timely basis, no procrastinating

    accept problems and difficulties as a part of life and deal with them

    occasionally risk going against the current

Angelaeon Circle type 9 characters:

King Laetham, introduced in *Breath of Angel*

Haden, introduced in *Eye of the Sword*

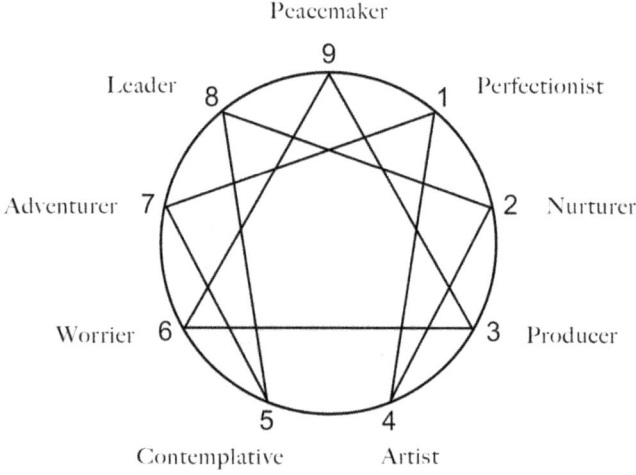

23.

The Option to Go Deeper

As you can see, the nine types allow you to create complex characters. But real people are much more complicated, so if you want, you can dive even deeper by extending your character's type into one of their neighboring types. In other words, a Type 3 person will naturally lean toward either a 2 or a 4. She's definitely an Achiever, craving success and avoiding failure, but she may also have some of the Nurturing traits of a Type 2. Or she may lean the other way and have some traits of the Artist, the Type 4.

For example, I definitely fit into Type 5. I value knowledge and wisdom, and I enjoy solitude, and I'm an observer. So I recognize most of my traits in the Contemplative of Type 5. But I also have a few traits described in the Type 4 Artist, such as creativity and a sensitivity to symbolism and the unseen.

So if you want to deepen your character, here's a look at the possible combinations. These side traits can also provide a few more options for backstory and motivation.

TYPE 1:
PERFECTIONIST - REFORMER - RENOVATOR

May lean toward 9: Peacemaker – Diplomat – Mediator

Or may lean toward 2: Nurturer – Helper – Caregiver

TYPE 2: NURTURER – HELPER – CAREGIVER

May lean toward 1: Perfectionist - Reformer - Renovator

Or may lean toward 3: Producer – Achiever – Ace

TYPE 3: PRODUCER – ACHIEVER – ACE

May lean toward 2: Nurturer – Helper – Caregiver

Or may lean toward 4: Artist – Individual – Romantic

TYPE 4: ARTIST – INDIVIDUAL – ROMANTIC

May lean toward 3: Producer – Achiever – Ace

Or may lean toward 5: Contemplative – Observer – Thinker

TYPE 5:
CONTEMPLATIVE – OBSERVER – THINKER

May lean toward 4: Artist – Individual – Romantic

Or may lean toward 6: Worrier – Skeptic – Doubter

TYPE 6: WORRIER – SKEPTIC – DOUBTER

May lean toward 5: Contemplative – Observer – Thinker

Or may lean toward 7: Adventurer – Bon Vivant – Zealot

TYPE 7: ADVENTURER – BON VIVANT – ZEALOT

May lean toward 6: Worrier – Skeptic – Doubter

Or may lean toward 8: Leader – Authority – Director

TYPE 8: LEADER – AUTHORITY – DIRECTOR

May lean toward 7: Adventurer – Bon Vivant – Zealot

Or may lean toward 9: Peacemaker – Diplomat – Mediator

TYPE 9: PEACEMAKER – DIPLOMAT – MEDIATOR

May lean toward 8: Leader – Authority – Director

Or may lean toward 1: Perfectionist - Reformer - Renovator

A WORD ABOUT CULTURE:

Having originated in ancient wisdom, the Enneagram is said to be universal. But there are other personality traits that tend to be more culturally specific, such as introversion and extroversion. Susan Cain, in her book *Quiet*, reports that Asian cultures tend to be introverted. They see themselves as part of a greater whole, honoring relationships within the family, the business, and the community. Western cultures honor the individual and personal destiny. Europe is more extroverted than Asian cultures, and the United States has some of the most extroverted people of all.

Again the bottom line is, if you are unsure about a particular culture, do your homework so that your characters accurately reflect their culture.

Part Three

Plot, Scene, and Emotions

24.

Conflict, Plot, and Scene

BEFORE WE GO ON, I want to point out some dangers:

1. HOLDING TOO RIGIDLY TO A SET OF TRAITS.

I mentioned this in regard to the stages of development in Part One. It also holds true for personality traits. The Enneagram allows me to see my characters as real people. Through their types I gain a feel for the who, how, and why of their lives. But while I'm all for writing character bios built on personality type and age, I don't believe in using that information to religiously measure each step my characters take. Instead, I prefer to hand over their bios to my muse and let the bios inform my imagination as I write. So once I've done personality and backstory work, I set aside their bios and simply write, trusting that I know my characters well enough to let them lead me through the story.

In other words, armed with what I know, I can write their scenes by instinct. If I get stumped, or if I'm unsure of how a character would realistically respond in a situation, I can always reread his bio. In fact, as my novel takes shape, I may even discover issues that send me back to rework his backstory or tweak his personality.

I'm just saying don't chain yourself to these stages and traits. Inform yourself and then give your muse free rein.

2. Focusing on the negative.

Have you ever stopped reading a novel that had a whiny protagonist? I have. Whiny, rude, crude ... if a protagonist doesn't give me a reason to like and care about her within the first few chapters, I stop reading. But as a writer, I can see how easy it is to make the mistake of emphasizing the negative. Especially if I'm concentrating on my character's stages and traits and figuring out her internal struggles. I rub my hands together in delight, hissing, "Yes! My protagonist is insecure. She's scared of failure, but masks it. Her snark serves to support her fragile self." I know my character's struggles, faults, and failures, so it's easy to write them into scene after scene. But if I weigh her down with too much of the negative, I end up making her unlikable. A protagonist should be flawed, yes, but as screenwriter Blake Snyder says, "liking the (character) we go on a journey with is the single most important element in drawing us into the story." So don't forget to make your protagonist likable.

To *likable*, author James N. Frey adds *courageous*. He believes that for the reader to like and identify with the protagonist, the character must show courage. "He either has (courage) to start with," Frey says, "or [he] finds it in the course of the story." I believe the best character-driven stories are always about the protagonist being squeezed until he is forced to find the courage to remove his mask and live without it.

3. WRITING EVERYTHING YOU KNOW ABOUT YOUR CHARACTER INTO THE STORY.

You now know much more about your character than you'll ever need to put into your book. Some of his backstory will be so interesting that you can hardly stand to leave it out. You may want to explain every bit of how he came to fear failure or crave understanding or feel compelled to help people. But to keep readers engaged, we can't slow down to dump all the backstory on them. Every time we pause to recount backstory or explain why our character became this type of person, we risk losing the reader. Remember the basic advice about backstory: Include it only if it's something the reader *must* know. Even then, don't use it until it answers a question or serves a purpose.

Conflict

So far we've focused on the factors involved in a character's internal conflict based on her stage in life and personality type. Her internal conflict comes from within as she struggles to keep wearing her emotional mask. Meanwhile, the external conflict forces her toward taking the mask off. What should that external conflict be? Your protagonist's bio has something to do with that as well.

What if you already have the external conflict in mind before you begin writing your novel, and you just need to flesh out your protagonist? In that case, you can go to the Enneagram and ask, "What kind of person would find the stakes in this conflict extremely high? What mask would find this situation a challenge?"

But what if you begin writing with a character in mind, and you're trying to sculpt the external conflict? If you know your protagonist's personality type, you can ask, "What kind of conflict would be a life-changing challenge for her? What outer circumstances would force her to deal with her mask and ultimately compel her to find the courage to remove it?" The major external conflict is the basis for the external arc of the plot.

Out of all your characters, your protagonist should have the most at stake, and her external goal should appear to be unattainable, whether it's opening up a bakery or climbing Mount Everest or escaping from behind enemy lines. It also needs to be personal and extremely important to your protagonist. Rachel Ballon, author of the wonderful book

Breathing Life into Your Characters, advises us to give our protagonists "a goal that they *desperately have* to reach. The more desperate the goal, the more *intensity*. The more opposition or obstacles that stand in the way, the more *conflict*. The greater the inner desire to reach the goal, the greater the *emotions*."

Our character's inner conflict is linked to her stage in life and her personality type. Dig into her backstory, and ask what still has a grip on her mind and emotions? What is she trying to forget? What are the emotional secrets she is struggling to keep hidden? Her internal conflict will form the internal arc of the plot.

So now we have internal conflict and external conflict, which both escalate as your protagonist moves forward, coming up against obstacles that keep her from reaching her goal and force her to grapple with her fears. Obstacles can come from nature, society, culture, technology, government, and, more to our focus here, other characters. "The meeting of two personalities is like the contact of two chemical substances," said Carl Jung, "if there is any reaction, both are transformed." If you know the traits of all your major characters, you can easily create conflict. Throw two or three or four of them together, and, just as in real life, agendas clash, even when all the characters in the scene are on the protagonist's side. Think Sherlock Holmes and Dr. Watson.

So in every scene, whether your secondary characters are for, against, or neutral to your protagonist, you can use what you know about them to create tension of some kind. Make sure your characters' motivations are at odds. They're working at cross purposes. They won't let their masks slip. They rub each other the wrong way. Maybe they argue. Or there's icy silence. Or they speak politely, but the subtext tells you that shark-size problems lie in wait just below the calm surface. Even minor conflict creates tension. And tension is what we want. Tension keeps readers reading.

As I mentioned before, my fantasy novels have large casts, which are easier to handle if I use the Enneagram. But speaking from experience, I suggest that you create as few characters as you can. Agent Donald Maass advises writers to make a list of characters and the roles each one plays. Then ask if any of the characters can be deleted. Can you combine two or more characters into one who does double duty? Or triple duty? Following that advice, I tried to work with as few characters as possible. A smaller cast really does make a story clearer and easier to tell. And I discovered that combining two characters into one sometimes creates surprising links or twists and can tighten loose ends in a plot.

PLOT

Lisa Cron, on writerunboxed.com, wrote, "... zeroing in on the story we're writing, *and the specific internal change the plot will be designed to put our protagonist through,* couldn't be more important. If we fail to do this work upfront, it's kind of like writing a book about a significant event in the life of someone who you know nothing about. Writing blind is dangerous because it tends to strand writers." (Italics mine.)

Writing blind is also dangerous because readers and reviewers are *not* blind. Here's how some Publishers Weekly book reviewers describe deficient plots.

"predictable plotting"

"plot points that strain credibility"

"the novel suffers from poor plotting"

"the action seems like much ado about very little"

"the action isn't anchored by sympathetic characters . . . simplistic moralizing"

"relying on stereotypical tropes and relatively elementary plot development. . . as predictable as it is repetitive with few, if any, surprises to distinguish it from countless other variations on the theme"

"the obviousness of the plot and a transparent moralistic message obscure and diminish the underlying concept"

If we turn these critiques into advice for our own plots, we can see that we're aiming for:

Action anchored by sympathetic characters (in other words, what happens is an integral part of the story and occurs for good reason)

Unpredictable or surprising plotting

Believable plot points

A plot rooted in issues that matter to both the protagonist and to readers

A message that grows naturally out of the story, not a story written to convey a message

In my opinion, well-written characters are the key to avoiding these types of plot problems. Believable characters make for believable plot points and can provide fresh, surprising plot developments. Well-motivated characters also make action happen for good reasons. In other words, events don't simply happen *to* the characters but *because of* the characters.

So let's say you know your basic story idea and your characters. Maybe you even have a rough draft, but it feels loosey-goosey. Either way, you've thought about age characteristics and personality types, and you know your characters better. Now you want to anchor everything. What next? I suggest thinking about the structure of your novel. Having a structure in mind will help you write and arrange your scenes – or rewrite and rearrange them. Again, characters are key. As Lisa Cron says, you "must create plot points driven by the protagonist's inner struggle if you want your story to go anywhere."

Plot points, which some writers call turning points, are pivotal external events and/or inner realizations that function as springboards to send the character onward. If characters were explorers, we could say plot points are the milestones they reach, places where they hammer a stake into the ground to show how far they've traveled toward their goal.

As for the overall journey, that's the plot. And just as there may be a variety of ways to map a journey, there are a variety of ways to structure plot. Robert McKee covers the subject of structure well in his book *Story*, so I won't describe all the types. But I will take you through the one structure that has helped me the most, and I'll show you how knowing your characters can help you plot your novels.

When I first got a Kindle e-reader, it bugged me that instead of page numbers, it had a segmented line across the bottom with location numerals to indicate the percentage of the book I had read. (I don't know if the new Kindles are like that or not, because I still have my old one.) Then I discovered that the percent-read line gives me, as a novel writer, an interesting overview of plot points. Having studied the three-act structure of story, I knew that a major plot point usually occurs approximately a quarter of the way into the story – at about 25%. So as I read e-book novels, I took note of where the percentage line was. Sure enough, around the 25% mark, a major plot development happened, pivoting the story into its second act, its middle.

Now in a traditional three-act structure, the first act generally covers 25% of the story, the last act covers 25%, and the middle or second act, is twice as long: 50%. I actually find four acts easier to plot. (I learned this from Beth Revis; I list links in the final chapter.) It's similar to the three-act structure, except that with four-acts, the middle is divided into two parts with a pivotal point at 50%.

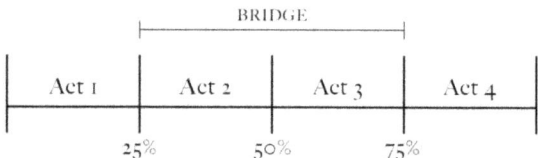

Either way, three-act or four, the first pivotal plot point comes about a fourth of the way into the story. That's where the characters begin crossing the bridge, the long middle space where most of the story happens. But what happens during the first 25% to get our characters to the bridge?

Here's where character traits and motivations come in, because a plot is not simply *what* happens but *why*. Yes, sometimes an event happens out of the blue, some coincidence with no why to it, like a storm or other "act of God" type of event. But if you want to keep your plot anchored and believable, you can't use many of those unmotivated events. Notice when you read well-written novels: If there is a coincidence, it usually occurs right at the beginning to kick things off – or it's the threat looming over the entire plot, causing major suspense (like an asteroid heading toward earth or a volcano threatening to erupt). Everything else must happen for a good reason. That means everything your characters think, say, and do must have a motivation. And motivation is anchored firmly in the personality type of each character.

No one wants to read about a character whose life is peaceful and smooth, all's well, fine and dandy. Where's the story in that? We want to see conflict. So during Act 1, the protagonist's life gets thrown out of balance. The first spot where this occurs is what screenwriter Michael Hauge calls "The Opportunity" or Turning Point #1.

So what would throw your protagonist off balance? Think of his personality type. What does he want above all else? He wants whatever bolsters his values, fits his personal goal and desire, and allows him to keep his "mask" on. What does he avoid at all costs? He avoids anything that challenges his values, goals, and desires; anything that threatens to reveal what's behind his mask. In short, he wants life to stay balanced (as he sees it) and wants to avoid anything that might throw him out of balance. Unfortunately for your protagonist, your job as a writer is to do the opposite. You must throw him out of balance and keep him there for most of the plot.

Human nature is to return anything unbalanced back to a balanced state, whether it's a picture on the wall or a relationship out of kilter. So when the inciting incident throws your protagonist off balance, she tries to regain balance. But it's also human nature to take the easiest path, which may be to ignore the imbalance and hope it restores itself. So maybe instead of taking "the opportunity" afforded by Turning Point #1, your protagonist denies that life is out of balance. In fact, she may vacillate for a while, worrying, "Do I deal with this issue or not?" But you won't let her swing back and forth for long. You'll push her until she is forced to deal.

So then what will she do? The next easiest thing. That means she'll deal with the problem the way she usually copes with problems. Her usual way is related to her weakness or "flaw," which is the immature response, the one that allows her to maintain her "mask." Of course, her usual way of coping only makes matters worse, which sends the plot off and running toward Turning Point #2, at which *Something* happens that forces her to try to resolve the issue in a different way, challenging her to grow emotionally (the internal arc) as the events of the story challenge her to make decisions and take action (the external arc). Hauge calls this "The Change of Plans." At this point, the stakes must be big enough for her to overcome her reticence to change. And whatever that is must be believable. That *Something*, a pivotal plot point, ends Act 1 (the first 25%) and ushers the story onto the bridge we call the Middle.

Writing Deep, Believable Characters

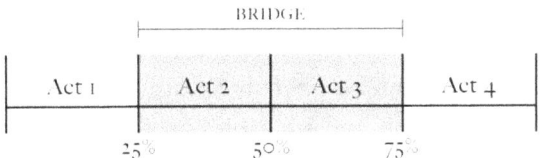

The Middle takes up approximately the next 50% of the story and is full of push and pull as the protagonist struggles to make progress in bringing balance to her life. But every time she thinks she has the problem in hand, the opposition sets her back. And each time she's set back, she responds. How? The usual responses to strong opposition (conflict) are fight or flight, and there are a variety of ways to do each. Your character's personality type will give you ideas for how she might respond. For more specifics I recommend Rachel Ballon's *Breathing Life into Your Characters*. She has a great discussion of fight or flight. But whether your character fights or tries to flee, she will respond both externally and internally.

With that in mind, let's move our protagonist across the bridge. In the four-act structure that I use, Act 2 is the second 25%, the first half of the long Middle. This is where some characters and circumstances line up to support our protagonist's cause, while others gather to undermine her. She begins to learn more about the plot problem and tries different ways to deal with the imbalance. Halfway through Act 2, there's a minor turning point: a connection is made or something bad happens, maybe something is discovered or revealed or foreshadowed. In any case, the stakes rise. To make progress now, your protagonist will have to start easing off her mask, but she'll do it reluctantly.

Each choice the protagonist makes should be significant and cause something else to happen. The same holds true for all other characters. Each acts and reacts according to his personality type and maturity level, and every action brings about a reaction. Everything is connected, cause and effect, throughout the whole story.

About 50% of the way through the novel, there's Turning Point #3, which Hauge calls "Point of No Return." Again, it can be a disaster or setback, a connection, discovery, or revelation. Whatever it is, it raises the stakes once more. But at this point, our protagonist is in so deep there is no turning back. As Beth Revis says, "If at this point you called Time Out, things couldn't go back to the life she had before."

At this point, we move into Act 3, the second half of the Middle, where everything escalates and presses in on our protagonist: events happen faster, opposition grows stronger, obstacles are more difficult to overcome. And if she tries to put her mask back on, she discovers it no longer fits. There's now more push and pull, more cause and effect – not thrown in just for the sake of effect but growing out of choices made previously by both protagonist and antagonist. Midway through Act 3, there's another minor plot point, a turn in the path that makes things look bleaker for both the outward goal and the emotional arc.

Now you're working toward the end of the middle. Your protagonist is facing serious difficulty, and the odds are mounting against her. Maybe supporters desert her or enemies gain the upper hand. Or both. You're headed toward the last step that moves your story off the Middle bridge and into the last act. And that step is a doozy. It's Turning Point #4, the "Major Setback." Victory, whether it's physical, relational, or emotional, looks further away than ever. The antagonist appears to have won. Emotionally, our protagonist's mask is down, but she's struggling to find any sort of balance, and she's failing. And then . . .

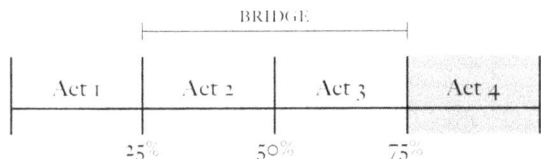

Expecting to lose, your protagonist steps off the bridge into Act 4 to face down her fears. This leads to what's called the "obligatory scene." That simply means that the big issue (or antagonist) you set up for her in Act 1 is what she is obligated to face at the climax in Act 4. This is your protagonist's point of "death," of self-sacrifice and heroism. She chooses to face her greatest fear, lets go of the last vestige of her mask, and willingly allows what she feared internally to have the upper hand. For example, the protagonist who has avoided failure now decides to allow herself to fail.

Why would she do that? That's what you have to set up, nudge her toward, and take her through. That "point of death" is Turning Point #5, the Climax. It's win or lose. Your choice. But however you play it out, it has to be believable and make sense according to the emotional arc and growth of your protagonist.

Act 4 takes up approximately the last 25% of the novel. Much of that time will be spent getting your protagonist to the obligatory scene and forcing her to face down her fear, both physically and emotionally. But after that, you'll need to show her returning to her new normal. This often echoes the beginning of the novel, but it shows how she has changed because of all you've put her through. Let readers see what life will be like for her in the coming days.

You've probably seen plot diagrams that look like a hill, where the external arc (the action) ascends as the obstacles get harder. Sometimes what's missing in those diagrams is the internal arc. As the external arc ascends, the internal arc should descend. That's because as outward pressure increases, your protagonist is forced to dig deeper into her emotional issues. "What happens *to* the character is not as important as what happens *inside* the character," says Rita Williams-Garcia. "What happens *to* the character is a catalyst for what happens *inside* her." It's most effective if your protagonist's internal arc reaches its lowest point roughly at the same time that the rising external dramatic action reaches its peak.

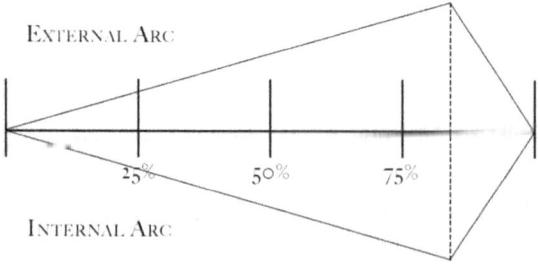

Now think of that diagram in terms of the personality type you've chosen for your protagonist. You know the way she thinks and acts when she is immature, and you know the mask she hides behind. That's the way she will start her emotional journey through the story. Thanks to the Enneagram, you also know what she needs to learn in order to mature, and you know you'll have to put her under pressure to get her there. That's the descending line of the internal arc. You also know what she'll be like when she's mature. She won't be perfect, but she won't need her mask any longer. That's the ascending line of the internal arc, which mirrors in reverse the denouement of the plot.

What I've just given you is all based on a four-act structure, and as I said before, there are many different ways to structure a novel. The point is, however you structure your novel, knowing your characters will only make it easier to create the story you want to tell.

I also want to emphasize that I'm not suggesting that you write by a formula. The best writing in any genre or non-genre is not formulaic. The worst writing is. What I'm giving you here is structure, not formula. It's up to you to avoid cliché and concoct fresh, surprising plots with fresh, surprising characters. Read, read, read, and study how other authors do this. Then write, rewrite, rewrite, and do it yourself.

Scene

The characters you need to know best are your protagonist and any other point of view characters. But your major secondary characters need to get the full treatment as well, especially your antagonist. As screenwriter Michael Hauge says, "Even the nemesis must be given qualities that will make him unique, interesting, and perhaps sympathetic." For minor allies and enemies, you can get away with sketchier character studies, but the more you understand them, the easier it will be to instinctively know how they will talk, act, and react in any given scene.

Scenes should be like falling dominoes: the first taps the next, which makes it fall, and so on in a chain reaction of cause-and-effect throughout the novel all the way to The End. What happens in one scene becomes an inciting incident for a later scene, and what happens in that later scene then becomes an inciting incident for subsequent action. *All of it* depends on the choices your characters make, and the choices they make depend on their personality types.

Each scene is a mini-plot with a beginning, middle, and end. The scene plot can be drawn in a mini-arc that looks like the external/internal arc of a novel. What drives this mini-arc is the conflict surrounding the point of view character's goal in the scene. And that conflict is sparked by friction between the character and opposing forces, often other characters. Here's where the different character types really get to shine.

"Treat all your secondary characters like they think the book's about them," advises writer Jocelyn Hughes. As it is in real life, so it is in believable fiction: each of us is the main character in our own life. So each character has his own logical, believable reason for being in that scene (if he does not, he shouldn't be there). He enters the scene with his own desires and fears, his own point of view and worldview, and his own agenda. As you write a scene, then, keep in mind not only how the situation looks to the scene's main character but also how it looks from the viewpoint(s) of the other character(s). Know what your point of view character hopes to accomplish in that scene, but also be aware of what the other characters hope to accomplish. That's where a large part of the conflict is created.

What if all the characters in the scene are on the same "team"? Each one still brings his or her own viewpoint and personality into the scene. As a result, what they say and do will reflect their personal agendas. Even if the only two characters in a scene are your protagonist and an ally, their individual agendas will differ enough to spark tension. For example, maybe the main opposition is a flooded stream blocking their way back to camp. Your main character wants to find a way across as soon as possible. His ally tries to persuade him to turn back and shelter in a cave. Their conflict is the fulcrum for a seesaw of wills, a tug-of-war between agendas. In this case it's we've-got-to-risk-it versus we've-got-to-stay-safe.

A scene, then, shifts between competing agendas. Back and forth it goes as the different personalities push and pull, responding to events and to each other until the turning point, the scene's climax, at which time everything shifts one more time and settles that way (at least for the time being). A scene's turning point can be a revelation, a discovery, a realization, a disaster, or a surprising turn of events. It sounds like big stuff, but the turning point does not have to be huge or earth shattering. In fact, some scenic turning points should be low-key or quiet and thoughtful. Even then, they can still carry tension. But whether the turning point is spectacular or subdued, it must reflect the change occurring in the scene.

One of the most important changes should occur in the scene's viewpoint character. If he entered the scene confident, he leaves uncertain. If he entered uncommitted, he leaves committed. It's a positive to negative or a negative to positive change. And don't forget his mask. He's either letting the mask drop a little more, or he's raising it again to protect himself. However you work it, there must be a change, large or small. If nothing changes, the scene is wasted time, spinning the plot wheels without going anywhere. Your job as a writer is to keep the story moving forward. Always.

So each scene in your novel should link in some way to both the internal and external journeys of your main character and carry him closer to achieving – or failing to achieve – the goal of the plot. Knowing your characters' personalities should make it easier to make those scenes believable as you recognize each character's agenda and spot potential conflicts that you can use to your advantage.

What if you have a large cast, and you've written several characters into one scene? How can you keep them straight and avoid confusing the reader? This is another good reason to know your characters. Poet and writer Nikki Grimes is a master at creating a variety of characters. (Her *Bronx Masquerade* is a great example.) She says, "When you view the characters as real people, it's fairly easy to keep the different voices straight."

One way to avoid confusion in a scene with several characters is to limit dialogue or action to about three characters at a time. If others join in, make it clear who is entering the conversation or the fray, and slip them in as naturally as possible.

I've given you only the basics here. There is much more involved in writing scenes. If you're interested in a deeper look, I recommend Sandra Scofield's *The Scene Book*.

25.
Emotional Impact

"PEOPLE REMEMBER the emotional context of a book – even if they read for plot," said Gennifer Choldenko (*Al Capone Does My Shirts*). And Agent Donald Maass says, "When you shape your reader's emotional journey—vary and progress it—your reader's experience will be rich, rewarding and memorable. A clever premise will hook. A nifty plot will intrigue. A strong arc will make a character interesting though not necessarily lovable. But take readers on an emotional journey and you will have their hearts in your hands."

But the fact is, you can't take your readers on an emotional journey unless your characters are on an emotional journey. That's a lesson I learned – and one I'm still learning – the hard way. My agent is always quick to flag places in my manuscripts where I fail to create the emotional impact a scene needs. So I pay attention to any advice I find about creating emotional impact. One thing I've discovered: Emotional impact is not something you embroider on top of a scene. It's woven into the fabric of the story. It's in the original threads. It's what makes a story a good story. And it grows out of character.

Here's what happens when we ignore the emotional journey. The following comments come from *Publishers Weekly* reviews that zero in on emotion – or rather the lack of it.

> "characters lead generic emotional lives that play out in the confines of a generic suburban drama"

> "underdeveloped emotions"

> "the resolution lacks the emotional impact it aims for"

But here's what happens when you get it right. This one is from a starred review:

> "Their (characters') voices reverberate with honesty, vulnerability, and deep emotions and will leave a lasting impression on readers."

I know which of the above reviews I'd rather receive. The good news is that knowing our characters allows us to access their emotions. We know their greatest fears, their highest hopes, their deepest desires, and their values. And ". . . values are by definition emotional," says writer Carol Bly. "[T]hey are how we *feel* about the given subject." So if we know what our characters value, we know what they *feel* about life: what frustrates them, what pleases them, what gives them a sense of identity, what leaves them confused and empty. Emotions reflect who our characters are. Even controlling beliefs grow out of strong convictions, and strong convictions come with strong emotions.

So, armed with what we know about the stages of life and personality types, how do we write stories that strike a strong emotional chord?

First, what not to do

Knowing a character's personality, we know what disappoints her. But simply saying, "she was sad" does not make a reader feel her sadness. Neither does an overabundance of drama-queen theatrics: weeping and wailing and flailing. That's melodrama, also known as sentimentality. "[S]entimental art uses stock character and emotions to try to conjure up those emotions," said author Annie Dillard. "To sentimentalize something is to savor rather than to suffer the sadness of it," wrote Frederick Buechner. It's "to sigh over the prettiness of it rather than to tremble at the beauty of it ..."

Here are four ways to tell real drama from melodrama, and they all have to do with character.

1. Stereotype

The hero who can do no wrong, the helpless damsel in distress, the totally evil villain – flat characters like these create melodrama. They're stereotypes, game pieces the writer moves around on the board of his story. You could switch out the game pieces for any others of the same stereotype, and it would make no difference. Note that stereotypes are different from archetypes. Archetypes are the roles characters may play in a story – hero or villain or sidekick – but the characters in those roles are multi-dimensional, not stereotypes. You could not switch them out, because the story grows out of who they are. There would be no story without them and their . . .

2. Motivation

Ronald Tobias, in *20 Master Plots and How to Build Them*, says melodrama occurs "[w]hen the emotion being expressed is beyond the subject matter's ability to sustain that level of emotion." So emotions should fit the situation, the character, and his motivation. "Melodrama is not the result of over-expression, but of under motivation; not writing too big, but writing with too little desire," says Robert McKee in *Story*. "The power of an event can only be as great as the sum total of its causes. We feel a scene is melodramatic if we cannot believe that motivation matches action."

3. Depth

"Melodrama is almost always about the external and superficial. Melodrama is shrieking vs. the quiet and deep truth of drama," says Les Edgerton in *Hooked*. Over-the-top emotional responses tend to be melodramatic. With real drama, even a scene that has little external action can be emotionally deep. It's the depth of the character's interior response that hooks the reader. Even then, the reader won't buy it if the timing is wrong.

4. Timing

To be effective, emotional responses must be earned. If they're not, the moment turns into melodrama. Let's say a story opens with a woman standing at a window, screaming at a man who is walking away. Even if we're given her name or told she's a mother, we don't know her, so it's hard to relate. We're not feeling her emotions, we're simply observing. We may want to know why she's screaming, but we don't really empathize with her yet.

Karl Iglesias in his book *Writing for Emotional Impact* emphasizes the need to build to an emotional punch. In real life an explosion of anger or an outburst of grief may surprise us, but we know these expressions of emotion don't come out of nowhere. The anger grew from a much lower level of irritation. And according to the stages of grief, the grieving process begins with denial. So build toward a believable emotional response.

Plotting the circumstances is key. "You can't expect your readers to feel what your protagonist feels just because your protagonist feels it," says Donald Maass in *21st Century Fiction*. "Only when that emotion is provoked through the circumstances of the story will your readers feel what you want them to."

WHAT TO DO

1. CARE ABOUT YOUR PROTAGONIST, AND DON'T ALLOW HER TO BE PASSIVE.

Part of what makes us care is seeing a character in action. She can't just let things happen to her. She has to push back and ultimately make the choices that drive the plot and solve the critical conflict. Even then, if her story doesn't move you emotionally, it won't move your readers. Of course, sometimes your story moves you and *still* isn't emotionally strong enough to affect the reader. In that case, it's probably a communication problem. *You* know and feel the emotion that drives the scene, but you haven't communicated it well. Which brings us to...

2. PUT YOUR OWN EMOTIONAL TRUTHS INTO YOUR STORIES.

Editor and novelist Peter DeVries said, "The writer can only explore the inner space of his characters by perceptively navigating his own." Emotions are attached to our experiences, so in order to access the fullness of an emotion, we may have to open a painful memory we've sealed away. When a scene should evoke emotion but doesn't, sometimes the reason is because the emotion is so personal and strong – or so recent and raw – that we are not allowing it to fully surface. We have to be willing to relive the feeling so it can flow into our characters.

3. SET THE TONE.

The beginning of a story should establish the mood or tone for what we're about to read. We should feel, early on, the emotional weight – light or heavy – of the story that's about to unfold. Then throughout the novel, the emotions will vary, roller-coastering to the end, but the reader should be able to get a sense of the emotional ride to come as soon as she steps on. What's more, readers need to know up front how the protagonist feels as she starts her journey so that they can feel it too. Then they can experience the emotional ups and downs with her.

4. SHOW, DON'T TELL.

This a Writing 101 guideline that I'm sure you've heard time and again. When I first started writing novels, I heard it too and thought I knew what it meant. I didn't. It's more complex than it sounds.

Here's what I knew (which I mentioned previously): Avoid telling the reader how the character feels. She was sad. He was worried. She was angry. As I said earlier, simply stating emotions does not evoke emotions in a reader. It's not that we can *never* say something like, "It saddened her." But for the most part we should "show her feelings," says Marion Dane Bauer. "Don't talk *about* what she feels, but see and feel it from her eyes."

I've given you lots of descriptors for each of the Enneagram types, like "she's meticulous" or "he's generous." It's up to you to show these emotions in action – or reaction as the case may be: She slumped to her chair. He rubbed the bridge of his nose as he paced. Her fist struck the table, making the teacups rattle. Think, too, about how her body is responding internally. We need to see and feel the physical sensations. A knot in her throat? Prickles up her spine? Sweaty palms?

We can also let the reader eavesdrop on her thoughts. Maybe she rationalizes. Maybe she contrasts her response to the way another character responds to the same event. Maybe she has a flashback. This is "show, don't tell" at its most basic.

But show-don't-tell is even more complex. It also means using active voice and avoiding the passive as much as possible. Passive voice places us at a distance; active voice moves us closer to the character. For example, instead of the passive "She was coaxed to step forward by the old woman's smile," rewrite it in active voice: "The old woman's smile coaxed her forward."

Watch out for words like "felt" and "saw." Instead of "she felt a shiver run down her spine," make it more immediate: "a shiver ran down her spine" or simply "she shivered." Instead of telling us, "she saw the ball of flame expand," show us: "The ball of flame expanded." Do whatever you can to believably keep the character – and the reader – on emotional alert.

But even showing emotion won't impact readers if they're not invested in the character's hopes, desires, and dreads. So . . .

5. Up the stakes.

In order for readers to care about the protagonist, writers have to make the stakes for this character credible and important. That's why we sometimes hear the advice: your protagonist should be the character who has the most at stake, the most to lose. Then throughout the plot, we raise the stakes. When we know a character's personality type, we have a better idea of how to raise the stakes to force her to remove her mask. If the stakes are realistic and she responds believably, then readers will get emotionally involved.

6. Use dialogue and subtext.

Dialogue shows emotion as it's filtered through a character's culture, age, and personality type. To create believable characters, it helps to hear each character's voice and personalized vocabulary. When he greets someone, is he formal or informal? When he agrees, does he say yep or yes, uh-huh, yeah, certainly, or of course? When he's puzzled, does he say, "I'm confused" or "That doesn't compute" or "Doesn't translate" or "Doesn't add up" or "Makes no sense" or "Makes about as much sense as snow in heat wave"? Of course, he may vary what he says according to who he's talking to – or will he? That depends on how your character reacts to the situation he is in.

"Voice is also shaped by the character's gender, age, education, occupation, geography (Where do they live? What country? Urban or rural?), time period, class, attitude, vocal patterns, their use of figurative language, and essentially every single thing they've ever experienced in their life!" said author Katrina Kittle in a guest post on writerunboxed.com. ". . . everything that makes up your character's real life informs the way she sees the world, and therefore informs the way she speaks. As you can see, voice, then, is deeply connected to characterization. It's so difficult to isolate one aspect of our craft from the others because they're all so braided together. Clear voice is aided by knowing your character inside and out."

But what does the character *not* say? That can be just as important. What does he avoid talking about? What is he glossing over? An entire conversation can take place in which what is *not* said – the subtext – expresses more than the actual dialogue. In that case, body language can help communicate the true emotion.

7. Use body language

This is also part of showing instead of telling. Now that you know your character's personality type, you can add small physical habits that hint at her emotions, like biting her nails or drumming her fingers when she's nervous. In her book *Snap*, Patti Wood points out ways that body language reveals thoughts and emotions. Even handshakes give a clue: "Hands get cold under stress," she says. Also "the palms of the hands sweat in response to stress." And what stresses your character? Whatever threatens her mask.

8. Use settings, specifics, senses, and symbols to support the emotions of a scene.

The place a character lives, where he works, and the transportation he uses can reflect his personality. Or if he's "masked," it may reflect the fact that he's hiding something. I recently read a novel in which the demeanor of one of the characters indicated that he was a cultured, well-educated man, but he chose to live in a small, run-down, unkempt trailer. That disparity signaled that something was going on under the surface.

Other setting elements can also support the emotion of a scene. Cliffs or caves or waves. Ripples in a pond or a glassy surface that mirrors the mountains. Storms, lightning, clear skies, wind. All can echo the emotion of your protagonist. So can smells and sounds and specific details – specific as in "garlic breath" instead of "bad breath" or "rose-scented" instead of simply "floral."

Symbols can convey emotion as well. Let's say you have a type 3 young adult character. Her goal is to be successful, which means she avoids failure. Red marks on school assignments make her feel ashamed; they mean she hasn't measured up. So red marks could be a symbol that implies failure and evokes a feeling of shame. You could use red pens, red x's, scratches, even a streak of red across the sky at sunset or a spill of ketchup to imply the emotion. (I've overdone it here to make my point. Use sparingly.)

What does the character carry in her pocket, backpack, bag or purse? What does she wear or refuse to wear? How does she decorate her room? You can make any of these a symbol of her emotional state.

Usually I don't think about symbolism until after I've written a first draft. As I reread I note any symbolic elements I might emphasize in one scene and also scatter into other scenes when I rewrite. But it's like adding spices to a stew. Symbols should add flavor but not be obvious and overpowering. So use symbols carefully and judiciously to subtly support your character's emotions.

9. Use complex or conflicting emotions within the point of view character.

According to Donald Maass, the best novels have tension on every page. But tension doesn't have to be bombastic. It can be micro-tension. In *The Fire in Fiction* he says, "...micro-tension has its basis not in story circumstances or in words, it comes from emotions and not just any old emotions but *conflicting emotions*." (my emphasis) If your protagonist is struggling to keep her mask on, she will naturally feel conflicting emotions.

10. **PAY ATTENTION TO PACING, BOTH AT THE PLOT LEVEL AND WITHIN SCENES.**

Creating emotional resonance is a matter of balance. Screenwriter Michael Hauge says, "Both the action and the humor lines [plot threads] should be alternately long and short: one to three scenes of heavy action or humor, followed by a few quieter or more serious scenes. This indicates the necessary peaks and valleys to the emotional level of your story." I don't take that statement as a formula but only as a reminder that a novel has a flow. To make the greatest emotional impact, we have to pay attention to creating ups and downs throughout the story. We also have to set up the big emotions and build to the turning points, which, in turn, should grow in intensity, increasing the emotional stakes all the way to the climax.

This is called *pacing*. As an example, think of jokes. A joke is a mini-story built around a set-up and a punch line. If the set-up is done right, the punch line evokes an emotional reaction – surprise, delight, laughter. Emotional impact in a novel is also created with a set-up that leads to a punch line (climax), which evokes a strong emotional response in the reader: tears, trembling, a gasp, a sigh of relief.

When I was working on emotional impact for one of my novels, I realized that the pacing was wrong. I had distributed several major emotional "hits" throughout the plot, which weakened the overall impact. In revision I consolidated the "hits" so that they culminated at about the same point. Then I wove threads through the plot and subplots to set up the hit.

I'm learning to grow emotional response at the scene level as well. Because a scene is a mini-story, it creates emotional response the same way: set-up and punch line. To pace the set-up, emotion at the start of the scene should be at its weakest. As the scene plays out, the emotion should grow, peaking at the turning point of the scene. That means the character enters the scene at a lower emotional intensity. Of course, that lower level could be at a two out of ten or at an eight out of ten. The point is, it will grow higher, or stronger through the scene.

If you, like me, are working on emotional impact, you may want to sketch out the emotional arc of important scenes. Here's my emotional sketch of a hospital scene in a novel that my agent is now pitching. I wanted to grow my main character's emotions from weak to strong in order to intensify the emotion to the breaking point, at which she slams out of the room and runs. In my plan I included options for non-verbal ways that my character might express her emotions. Once I had this sketch, I wrote the full scene, including dialogue that, along with action, helped express her emotion.

When the scene opens, Tani arrives at the hospital, where an ambulance has taken her mother. As she enters the waiting room, she is apprehensive. From there, her emotions grow:

tense

anxious (glancing at clock; shifting, unable to get comfortable, too hot, too cold, tight chest, insides quivering)

edgy

scared (hands jammed into armpits, sweat on lip or forehead, gulping breaths)

alarmed

overwhelmed (shaky hand to forehead, voice chokes, quakes, poor balance, muttering, sagging into chair, leaning on doorframe for support, glassy stare, glazed look, staring at empty palms, leaning over, hands on knees, light-headed, non-responsive)

crushed

defeated (hands limp, thick voice, backing away, clutching body as if to hold it together, vacant eyes, slumping into chair, holding head with hands, cracking voice, feel pulse in the throat, heart thuds dully, sour taste, painful lump in throat, limbs too heavy to move)

wretched

despairing (feverish, over-bright eyes, a pained stare, shaking one's head in denial, rubbing upper arms for comfort, sweating profusely, racing heartbeat, dry mouth)

devastated

This type of plan is not a paint-by-numbers kit but a guide to give me a general idea of where I'm going. I don't follow it exactly, nor do I use all the body language I listed.

If I did, the scene would feel either stiff and forced, or melodramatic, or both. With this plan, I'm simply trying to get an idea of my character's emotional trajectory. The list keeps me aware of how her emotion rises throughout the scene as well as how she might exhibit those rising emotions. I set aside the list to write the scene, referring to it only when I need help to remember how her feelings would escalate.

Pacing in a scene also has to do with how the dialogue flows, where you pause for interior monologue, and where you insert details about setting and action. There are no must-follow rules for pacing; it seems to be something you *feel* as you read. So after you've written the scene, read it aloud – or listen to someone else read it. Does the scene flow smoothly? Does your character accelerate emotionally from zero to sixty in five seconds, or does her emotion build, bringing the reader along with her? Does she peak at a four when her situation and her personality type call for a ten?

Author Sundee Frazier advised a group of writers to ask specific questions about emotions during revisions:

"What phrases enable you to feel what the main character is feeling? Underline with a squiggle. This is where you successfully conveyed her emotion. You want more lines like this.

"What phrases put a wall between you and the main character? Underline with a straight line. These spots can use work. Replace those phrases and draw us into your character's emotions.

"Put a check mark where you want to feel more and see more emotion. These places need attention as well."

And so ...

CHARACTER IS STORY, and story is character. But story and character are not worth much without emotion, because emotion is basic to real life. Readers are emotional beings, so whether your story is plot-driven or character-driven, readers come to it expecting an emotional experience – action-adventure excitement, sigh-worthy romance, belly laugh humor, hair raising horror, heart-soaring inspiration. If you can consistently offer readers what they want to feel, you'll have no trouble gaining a fan base. But in order to do that, *you* first have to experience the emotions. And so do the characters. Deeply and believably.

I hope this book has been helpful to you. If all else fails, simply still yourself and listen. As Rita Williams-Garcia says, "If you ever sit still long enough to hear your characters, they reveal themselves to you."

And don't forget to enjoy the process of character creation, because ...

> "[T]here is something wonderful about being able to get inside the skin of people unlike yourself."
>
> Lee Smith

26.

Helpful Books, Links, and References

THIS IS A LIST of books and links I highly recommend. (And I've not been paid to say so.) Some have influenced the direction I've taken in this book. Others are some of my favorite craft books. I include them in case you're looking for help or encouragement in areas besides character development.

Writing in general, including creating characters:

<u>Writing Fiction: A Guide to Narrative Craft</u>, Janet Burroway. Covers all aspects of the craft. A classic.

<u>Wired for Story</u>, Lisa Cron. How writers can appeal to readers based on the latest brain research that indicates that we are "wired for story."

Write Away, Elizabeth George. Focused on mystery; includes a helpful, detailed look at her process.

Story, by Robert McKee. Great info on all aspects, especially structure.

Writing the Breakout Novel and its workbook, Donald Maass.

Writing 21st Century Fiction, Donald Maass. Anything written by Maass is excellent. He is insightful and straightforward. No matter what level your writing, he will challenge you to go deeper, and your writing will be much better for following his prompts.

Creating characters:

Breathing Life into Your Characters, Rachel Ballon. Includes sections on dysfunction, disorders, and troubled personalities.

The Writer's Journey, Christopher Vogler. Approaches character from the model of archetypes found in the "hero's journey" with lots of examples from current books and movies.

Create a Character Clinic: A Step-by-Step Course in Creating Deeper, Better Fictional People, Holly Lisle. "Step by step" is the operative word here. All of Holly's courses lead you through detailed steps to achieve your writing goals.

Quiet: The Power of Introverts in a World That Can't Stop Talking, Susan Cain. An in-depth look at the traits of introversion and extroversion.

Troubled characters:

Heroes and Heroin: Writing a Character Who Has an Addiction, nailyournovel

The Power to Prevent Suicide: A Guide for Teens Helping Teens, Richard E. Nelson, Judith C. Galas, and Bev Cobain. Includes a list of 40 powerful stressors that affect teens. Helpful when you're looking for ideas for conflicts and pressures for young adults in your novel.

See also Breathing Life into Your Characters by Ballon, listed above.

Ages and Stages of Life Development:

Yardsticks, Chip Wood. An age by age look at specific characteristics of children age four through fourteen. Specifically for teachers, but also helpful for writers of children's books.

Childhood and Society, Erik Erikson. Includes his analysis of all the stages I covered in this book.

Theories of Human Development, Malcolm W. Watson. An audio course offered by The Great Courses. A deeper look at the most influential researchers and their theories.

Moral Development and Reality, John C. Gibbs. A bit scholarly, but if you're doing research, it's a good resource, building off of the work of Lawrence Kohlberg and Martin Hoffman.

Raising Good Children, Dr. Thomas Lickona. Lays out the stages of moral development; suggests ways to influence children toward positive moral choices. Down-to-earth, easy to understand. Useful for parents and teachers.

YPulse. Current research on youth culture.

THE ENNEAGRAM:

The Enneagram: A Christian Perspective, Richard Rohr, Andreas Ebert, Crossroad Publishing. An in-depth look at the nine personality types and how they interrelate. This was my primary source for Part 2.

Discovering Your Personality Type: The Essential Introduction to the Enneagram, Don Richard Riso, Russ Hudson. A basic introduction.

If you're interested in testing yourself to discover your Enneagram type, visit: http://enneagraminstitute.com

Plotting and scene:

The Scene Book, Sandra Scofield. Great book for understanding scene and how it works.

Hooked, Les Edgerton. How to create a compelling opening scene and inciting incident.

20 Master Plots and How to Build Them, Ronald Tobias

Beth Revis, writing advice on structure on wattpad and four-act structure.

Creating emotional resonance:

Writing for Emotional Impact, Karl Iglesias - Writers are "in the emotion-delivery business." And "write what makes you feel."

The Emotion Thesaurus, Angela Ackerman and Becca Puglisi. Seventy-five emotions detailed with suggestions for body language and inner mental and physical responses that signal each. Also includes writing tips for creating emotional resonance.

Snap, Patti Wood. Emotional responses and body language.

Writing for Story, Jon Franklin – Although this book is about writing nonfiction, its excellent advice on creating emotional impact translates into fiction writing as well.

<u>The Fire in Fiction</u>, Donald Maass. Great general writing advice with a strong emphasis on emotional impact.

<u>Getting Into Character</u>, Brandilyn Collins. An actor and novelist looks at how techniques for creating emotions onstage can help writers create believable emotions in their characters.

<u>Creating Character Emotions</u>, Ann Hood. Covers one emotion per chapter and shows examples of what works and what doesn't.

Encouragement:

I turn to these books again and again when I'm discouraged with my writing.

<u>Art and Fear</u>, David Bayles and Ted Orland.

<u>The War of Art</u>, Steven Pressfield.

Golden Rule texts from a variety of religions and cultures:

<u>scarboromissions.ca</u>

<u>wikipedia.org</u>

<u>unification.net</u>

References:

These are writers or researchers I've quoted or referred to in each chapter.

Chapter 1

Janet Burroway, <u>Writing Fiction: A Guide to Narrative Craft</u>.

Renee Swindle, guest post <u>"If Buddha Wrote a Novel"</u> on Writer Unboxed.

<u>Marion Dane Bauer</u>, lecture at <u>Vermont College of Fine Arts</u>, 2003.

Chapter 2:

<u>Anne Ursu</u>, anneursu.com

Malcolm Watson, <u>Theories of Human Development</u>.

Erik Erikson, <u>Childhood and Society</u>.

John C. Gibbs, <u>Moral Development and Reality</u>.

Chapter 3:

Jean Piaget as quoted in <u>A Piaget Primer: How a Child Thinks</u> by Dorothy G. Singer and Tracey A. Revenson.

James W. Fowler, Stages of Faith: The Psychology of Human Development and the Quest for Meaning.

CHAPTER 4:

Erik Erikson, Childhood and Society.

Jean Piaget as quoted in A Piaget Primer: How a Child Thinks by Dorothy G. Singer and Tracey A. Revenson.

Thomas Lickona, Raising Good Children.

James W. Fowler, Stages of Faith: The Psychology of Human Development and the Quest for Meaning.

Scott Spencer interview on "Fresh Air" on National Public Radio.

CHAPTER 5:

Erik Erikson, Childhood and Society.

Howard Gardner, The Unschooled Mind.

Thomas Lickona, Raising Good Children.

Robert Solomon, tape series No Excuses: Existentialism and the Meaning of Life. The Great Courses.

Chapter 6:

Chip Wood, <u>Yardsticks</u>.

Erik Erikson, <u>Childhood and Society</u>.

Jean Piaget as quoted in <u>A Piaget Primer: How a Child Thinks</u> by Dorothy G. Singer and Tracey A. Revenson.

Howard Gardner, <u>The Unschooled Mind</u>.

Thomas Lickona, <u>Raising Good Children</u>.

James W. Fowler, <u>Stages of Faith: The Psychology of Human Development and the Quest for Meaning</u>.

Chapter 7:

Chip Wood, <u>Yardsticks</u>.

Jean Piaget as quoted in <u>A Piaget Primer: How a Child Thinks</u> by Dorothy G. Singer and Tracey A. Revenson.

Daniel J. Siegel, <u>Brainstorm: The Power and the Purpose of the Teenage Brain</u>.

Daniel Goleman, interview in <u>What We Believe But Cannot Prove</u>, ed. John Brockman.

Thomas Lickona, <u>Raising Good Children</u>.

Chapter 8:

Marie Lamba in a guest post, Writers Digest online.

"The Merchants of Cool," wgbh Frontline, accessed 10/01/08.

David Kupelian, Selling Sex and Corruption to Your Kids, accessed 10/01/08.

Anastasia Goodstein of Ypulse, as quoted in "Teens Give Out MySpace Pages," USA Today, Monday, January 9, 2006.

Juliet Schor, Born to Buy.

Peggy Orenstein, Cinderella Ate My Daughter.

Jean Piaget as quoted in A Piaget Primer: How a Child Thinks by Dorothy G. Singer and Tracey A. Revenson.

Kevin Huggins, Parenting Adolescents.

Nelson, Galas, and Cobain, The Power to Prevent Suicide: A Guide for Teens Helping Teens.

Orson Scott Card, introduction to Speaker for the Dead, Tor 1991 edition.

James W. Fowler, Stages of Faith: The Psychology of Human Development and the Quest for Meaning.

Kelly Bingham, "Facing Life Head-On: Teen Protagonists," lecture at Southern Festival of Books, Fall 2008.

CHAPTER 9:

Deborah Halverson, "New Adult Fiction for the Young Adult Writer," Society of Children's Book Writers and Illustrators bulletin, Sept/Oct 2014

Erik Erikson, Childhood and Society.

Peggy Orenstein, Cinderella Ate My Daughter.

John C. Gibbs, Moral Development and Reality.

CHAPTER 10:

Erik Erikson, Childhood and Society.

CHAPTER 11:

Frederick Buechner, Listening to Your Life.

Erik Erikson, Childhood and Society.

Dan McAdams, quoted by Susan Cain, Quiet: The Power of Introverts in a World That Can't Stop Talking.

CHAPTER 12:

E. Mavis Hetherington and Ross D. Parke, Child Psychology.

Pierre Dasin quoted by Hetherington and Parke, ibid.

John C. Gibbs, <u>Moral Development and Reality</u>.

Chapter 13:

David C. Corbett, <u>The Art of Character</u>.

Mark Twain, "Pudd'nhead Wilson's New Calendar," <u>Following the Equator</u>.

James Scott Bell, <u>Plot and Structure</u>.

Chapters 14-22

The Angelaeon Circle novels: <u>Breath of Angel</u>, <u>Eye of the Sword</u>, and <u>Throat of the Night</u>.

Chapter 23:

Susan Cain, <u>Quiet: The Power of Introverts in a World That Can't Stop Talking</u>.

Chapter 24:

Blake Snyder, <u>Save the Cat</u>.

James N. Frey, <u>How to Write a Damn Good Mystery</u>.

Rachel Ballon, <u>Breathing Life into Your Characters</u>.

Carl Jung, <u>Modern Man in Search of a Soul</u>.

Donald Maass, <u>21st Century Fiction</u> and <u>The Fire in Fiction</u>.

Lisa Cron, <u>Wired for Story</u>.

Robert McKee, <u>Story</u>.

Beth Revis, <u>four act for writers</u> and <u>wattpad writing advice</u>

Michael Hauge, <u>Writing Screenplays that Sell</u>.

<u>Rita Williams-Garcia</u>, lecture at <u>Vermont College of Fine Arts</u>, January 2002.

Jocelyn Hughes, quoted on <u>Writers Write</u>.

<u>Nikki Grimes</u>, lecture at <u>Vermont College of Fine Arts</u> alumni conference, July 2014.

Sandra Scofield, <u>The Scene Book</u>.

CHAPTER 25:

Gennifer Choldenko, <u>keynote address</u> at the Society of Children's Book Writers and Illustrators Midsouth Conference, August 2014.

Donald Maass post <u>The Reader's Emotional Journey</u> on Writer Unboxed.

Carol Bly, <u>The Passionate, Accurate Story</u>.

Annie Dillard, Living by Fiction.

Frederick Buechner, Listening to Your Life.

Robert McKee, Story.

Ronald Tobias, 20 Master Plots and How to Build Them.

Les Edgerton, Hooked.

Karl Iglesias, Writing for Emotional Impact.

Donald Maass, 21st Century Fiction and The Fire in Fiction.

Peter DeVries as quoted by Rachel Ballon in Breathing Life into Your Characters.

Marion Dane Bauer, lecture at Vermont College of Fine Arts, 2003.

Katrina Kittle, guest post I'd Know That Voice Anywhere on Writer Unboxed.

Patti Wood, Snap.

Michael Hauge, Writing Screenplays that Sell.

Sundee Frazier, lecture at Vermont College of Fine Arts, 2004.

Rita Williams-Garcia, lecture at Vermont College of Fine Arts, January 2002.

Lee Smith as quoted in Writing Fiction: A Guide to Narrative Craft by Janet Burroway.

ABOUT KARYN HENLEY

I currently write young adult novels, both fantasy and contemporary, exploring coming-of-age issues that include questioning taken-for-granted beliefs, discovering romance, and dealing with the ripples our choices create. With an undergrad degree in education, I taught and wrote educational material for many years and conducted training seminars for teachers and parents. In 2004 I received an MFA in Writing for Children and Young Adults from Vermont College of Fine Arts. I have traveled extensively both in the U.S. and abroad. In addition to travel, I enjoy nature and pondering the mystery we call God. I believe that each person's life is a story with a beginning, a middle, an end, and an echo.

Novels by Karyn Henley

Breath of Angel

Eye of the Sword

Throat of the Night

for more information:

www.KarynHenleyFiction.com

www.ingramcontent.com/pod-product-compliance
Lightning Source LLC
Chambersburg PA
CBHW071608080526
44588CB00010B/1064